LAURA ASHLEY WINDOWS

LAURA ASHLEY
WINDOWS

ELIZABETH WILHIDE

HARMONY BOOKS
New York

Published by Harmony Books, a division of
Crown Publishers, Inc., 225 Park Avenue South,
New York, New York 10003 and represented in Canada by
the Canadian MANDA Group

Published in Great Britain by
George Weidenfeld & Nicolson Limited,
91 Clapham High Street, London SW4 7TA, England

Laura Ashley and logo
are trademarks of Laura Ashley Manufacturing BV

HARMONY and colophon
are trademarks of Crown Publishers, Inc.

Manufactured in Italy

Library of Congress Cataloging-in-Publication Data
Wilhide, Elizabeth.
    Laura Ashley windows.
    1. Windows. 2. Interior decoration. 3. Laura Ashley
(Firm) I. Title.
NK2121.W48 1988   747′.3   87-29328
ISBN 0–517–56754–7
    10 9 8 7 6 5 4 3 2 1
    First Edition

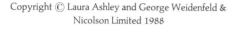

Contents

A History
of Windows

A HISTORY OF WINDOWS

Windows mediate between the interior and the world outside. By admitting light and fresh air, they make rooms habitable; by revealing views, they make rooms interesting. They form a frontier between one type of space and another.

The effect of windows – and window treatments – on interior design is profound, but windows are also integral to the overall style and structure of a building. The history of windows is in effect the history of architecture in miniature, reflecting technological advances and changes in artistic style.

The Ancient World

The civilizations of antiquity – Mesopotamia, Ancient Egypt, Greece and Rome – were established around the perimeter of the Mediterranean in areas where the climate is hot and light intense. The earliest buildings were not structurally sophisticated, relying on the mass of walls for strength, and so as not to weaken the entire fabric, apertures were generally small. These simple holes in roofs and deep, narrow clerestory openings in walls filtered the strong Mediterranean light and were perfectly adequate for ventilation, keeping the interiors cool.

As the column and beam, or post and lintel, method of construction evolved, resulting in the great temples of the classical world, windows could, in principle, be larger. But even such important and structurally sophisticated buildings as the Pantheon in Rome had quite small windows. In domestic buildings, windows were typically ranged around a central court or atrium; the two exterior walls were often entirely solid. Both town and country houses followed this pattern, but notable exceptions were the *insulae* or apartment blocks which had large windows facing both towards the streets and internal courtyards.

Most windows were uncovered. The process of heating sand, soda and lime to make a transparent material had been known since about 1500 BC but the use of glass was relatively rare. It was impure and therefore only semi-transparent, and it could not be made in large pieces. When windows needed to be covered for privacy, thin slabs of translucent marble, mica, animal skins, stone trellis or oiled paper were used instead. However, in the Roman *thermae*, or bath houses, windows were glazed in order to admit light but keep in the heat.

Mediaeval Europe

With the spread of civilization northwards into Europe and the impact of Christianity, institutional architecture changed fundamentally. In northern Europe, light is at a premium and there was a need for apertures to be larger. Increasingly, light in churches and cathedrals came to be linked with religious awe, as a manifestation of 'divine light'. These practical and spiritual considerations coincided with a development in masonry construction which

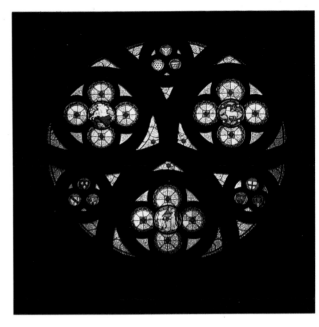

ABOVE *The magnificent 'wheel window' of St Mary's Church, Boyton, in Wiltshire with its decorative bar tracery. Large round stained glass windows typify mediaeval church architecture, and this example is a true tour de force of the art with its boldly geometric design and its brilliant, jewel-like colours.*

LEFT *The great hall of Penshurst Place in Kent is one of the largest of its kind in England. Built in 1341 for the merchant Sir John de Pultney, the hall remains to this day in its original mediaeval state. The exquisite gothic windows with their ecclesiastic tracery flood the hall with light, a delightful contrast to the massive stone walls.*

PRECEDING PAGES *A cottage scene painted by Ralph Todd in the 1880s shows a profusion of flowers around a casement window, and a simple lace curtain. By the nineteenth century glass was cheap enough to enable even the humbler householders to enjoy well-lit interiors.*

In the mediaeval interior, windows would have been screened with internal wooden shutters, sometimes decorated with simple patterns, but the most lavish display was reserved for tapestries and hangings, which were often richly embroidered. This scene, dated 1454, is a French illustration from Aristotle's Ethics.

allowed walls to be filled in with delicate traceries of stone, holding large leaded windows composed of many small and often coloured pieces of glass.

From the rounded arches of the Romanesque style to the rose windows and pointed arches of high gothic, solidity gradually gave way to soaring, fluid constructions. Stained glass had been used to great effect in Byzantine churches, but it reached a peak of magnificence in the gothic cathedrals of Europe. Chartres Cathedral (built between 1194 and 1260) is one of the most notable. The multicoloured jewel effect from its 160 windows, filled with thirteenth-century stained glass, dapples the interior surfaces. Beautiful and awe-inspiring, these windows told biblical stories in pictures, a practical necessity when illiteracy was widespread.

Cathedral building represents an architectural summit, fostered by the wealth and dominance of the Church, but such elaboration of structure and sophistication of window design was unknown in domestic building. From the days of the Roman Empire until the thirteenth century, the most common English house type was the aisled hall, which had an opening in the roof to let out smoke from the fire and narrow windows to give ventilation without sacrificing security.

By the thirteenth century, windows were larger and usually either pointed or rounded at the top, reflecting shapes used in ecclesiastical building. Although they were sometimes fitted with cross-bars or transoms, wooden shutters were still the most prevalent form of covering. In England, these were fitted internally, whereas in other European countries, particularly in Scandinavia, they were external, a protection against severe winter weather. Glass was expensive and could only be made in small pieces which had to be braced with lead to make a larger pane. It was a luxury item and only used in wealthier households.

Tudor and Elizabethan Developments

A general improvement in social conditions and growing prosperity in the fifteenth century, together with new methods of timber-frame construction, transformed house building. Windows were conceived as an integral part of the structure of walls and the use of glass became more common.

At first windows remained small and their heavy glazing bars obscured light, but there were radical developments in design in the early sixteenth century. Wrought-iron casement windows came into use, hinged onto either a stone or oak frame. The mullioned glass was fixed by means of lead strips in lattice, diamond and rectilinear patterns.

The quest for greater light in the interior led to those characteristic features of fifteenth-century buildings – oriel windows. Although still composed of small individual panes, the oriel window as a whole was large and projected out from the wall so that light came in from three sides. While early Tudor houses were often built around an inner courtyard and looked inwards, by Elizabethan times houses such as Longleat in Wiltshire and Gayhurst in Buckinghamshire were built with projecting bays facing outwards. This rapprochement with the surrounding landscape led to a vogue for formal planting and the well-designed view.

ABOVE *The oriel window, which projected from the wall and was glazed on all sides, was a fifteenth-century precursor of the later bay window and maximized the amount of light admitted into an interior.*

LEFT *Up until the seventeenth century and later, windows were often not curtained at all, light being at a premium, particularly in Northern Europe. This charming scene by the seventeenth-century Dutch genre painter Adrian van Ostade shows the dim light admitted by the irregular little panes of the leaded casement window.*

11

A symmetrical arrangement of square windows and projecting bays dominates the elevation of Longleat, in Wiltshire, built by Sir John Thynne in the late sixteenth century. The huge windows – which occupy more space than the stonework – are typical of the majestic, outward-looking façades of Elizabethan domestic architecture.

Windows were no longer pointed in the gothic style but gently arched or square-headed; these shapes were intended to lighten the interior. But glass still had a low transparency so windows were set in deep reveals, which were splayed or chamfered to improve the quality of light. Oriels or bays were as wide as possible, with the windows braced by cross-bars for strength.

From the Renaissance to Neo-classicism

The Renaissance was an immense and vital cultural movement, originating in Italy in the fifteenth century and spreading steadily throughout the rest of Europe over several centuries. The effects of the Renaissance were felt throughout the arts, but in architecture they were particularly pervasive, providing models of elegance and harmony unsurpassed today. Early manifestations in fifteenth- to sixteenth-century Italy were rigorously formal, based on the classical notions of order, symmetry and proportion, but by the seventeenth century a freer interpretation of classical rules became popular.

The most significant innovation in window design was the invention of the sash towards the middle of the seventeenth century. It changed the whole relationship between architecture and light, and typifies Renaissance precepts. The first sash windows (from the French *chassis*, or frame) consisted of two sections of window set in a frame. Only the bottom section moved, sliding up on

ABOVE *Angled bays or oriels were used not only for grand houses but also for more humble dwellings, such as this seventeenth-century cottage in Suffolk. The elaborate plasterwork is a local form of decoration known as pargetting.*

ABOVE RIGHT *The architects of the Georgian period, inspired by classical precepts of proportion, used windows to create rhythm and order. The rectilinear shape of the new sash window was subtly varied to define different storeys, with the tallest windows on the grand first floor, and the smallest, squarest windows for the servants' quarters at the top of the house. The expanses of glass to the left of this Georgian terrace would originally have been filled with wooden glazing bars, like those of its next-door neighbours.*

runners, and was held in place by catches or pegs at the side. By 1700 the sliding sash had been developed, with counterbalance weights concealed inside the frame and a system of cords and pulleys that enabled both halves of the window to slide freely up and down.

Although the sash window was rarely used in France, it was universally adopted in England and northern Europe. Leaded lights became outdated. Casement windows generally opened inwards and took up too much room; they were difficult to repair and to clean. Equally importantly, the whole style of the casement window was at odds with the new spirit of building.

Glass also improved in quality during the seventeenth century. A new manufacturing process enabled glass to be made in lengths of up to four feet; by 1701 'plate' glass six foot square could be produced, but it was very expensive. Nevertheless, panes became larger and wooden glazing bars much finer, giving windows a light, elegant appearance.

Tiers or pairs of interior shutters had simultaneously given way to more refined folding shutters, which fitted neatly into a recess in the window embrasure. The face panel was often decoratively painted. And some windows were not recessed at all, but simply set off with a classical architrave.

Clear mirror glass — a further Renaissance refinement — became a popular way of maximizing light. To create drama, mirrors were often set between pairs of windows or on the facing wall — as in the Hall of Mirrors at Versailles — thus providing the symmetry beloved of Renaissance architects.

ABOVE *Turner's watercolour sketch,* An Artist Painting in a Room with a large Fanlight *of c. 1828, shows an interior flooded with light from a huge arched window. Typical of the time, such windows were often extremely elegant, with fine glazing bars radiating out from the centre like the spokes of a wheel.*

RIGHT *The late eighteenth and early nineteenth centuries saw a fascination with the rustic idyll. In architecture this desire to move closer to nature was expressed in the many follies and decorative 'cottages' which sprang up around the carefully landscaped parks of wealthy landowners. Gothic detailing and pointed windows, as seen in this nineteenth-century cottage at Stourhead, were all part of the fantasy.*

In Britain, the effects of the Renaissance were slow to be felt. Eighteenth-century architects, influenced by the work of Inigo Jones (1573–1652), adopted the Palladian style evident in Italy two centuries earlier. The Earl of Burlington (1694–1753) was one of those responsible for introducing this restrained classicism to English taste. The proportion and distribution of windows were all-important elements. Subtle variations in the ratio of height to breadth gave facades character and distinction. Window shape also defined different storeys: windows on the *piano nobile*, where the main reception rooms were located, were twice as high as wide, while the squarest were at the top.

Apart from the standard sash, other Georgian window shapes included the Venetian or thermal window and the bow. The Venetian window consisted of a central arched window flanked by two smaller windows, aligned with the beginning of the arch. First adopted in grand houses in the early eighteenth century, they later became widely popular, although many strict Palladian designers found them too elaborate for their tastes. The bow window, an adaptation of the oriel, was fashionable late in the eighteenth century and on into the Regency period from 1810 to 1830. Together with the refinement of glazing bars, filigree work in fanlights and the use of ornament such as pediments, Georgian window design achieved a height of nobility and sophistication.

The eighteenth century saw the growth of middle class prosperity, and emphasis was placed on comfort and convenience alongside classical precepts. Speculative building transformed large cities; terraces of townhouses sprang up, often treated as a single stylistic composition to simulate a palace. Robert Adam (1728–92) and John Nash (1752–1835) both produced fine examples of this type of city development in London while the crescents and squares of Bath are also notable. But the homogeneity of Georgian architecture was not only due to pervasive neo-classical ideals but also to the effects of the 1667 Building Act

which established standards of house construction. These 'Rate Houses' were distinguished by size and by structure and laid the blueprint for expansion.

Another important piece of legislation was the Window Tax, first introduced in 1697 and levied at intervals until its repeal in 1851. Since the larger the house, the more windows its structure could support, the number of windows in a property was considered an effective scale by which to measure the status and wealth of a household. The tax capitalized on the popularity of the sash window and fell most heavily on the middle classes. Bricked up or blind windows, which can still be seen today, were an attempt to lighten the burden of the tax.

By the end of the eighteenth century, tall narrow sash windows had become almost universal. Elegant and of considerable size, they flooded the interior with light. Light, is important in mediaeval churches as a symbol of divine spirit, was now associated with the calm rationality of the age of enlightenment. Glass was now fully transparent and windows often incorporated window seats where people could sit to enjoy the view. The landscape was changing too; informal 'Picturesque' gardens and parks created romantic vistas which contrasted with the severe, symmetrical and disciplined lines of the architecture.

Nineteenth-century Revivals

At the turn of the nineteenth century, the momentum of classicism had dissipated into a general fascination with 'antiquarian' styles and exotica. Travel became easier and styles were often adopted after a Grand Tour. In addition to the Greek revival which formed the basis for the severe Empire style throughout Europe, ideas for shapes were borrowed from gothic architecture, from Ancient Egypt and even from China and India.

Window styles reflected this wealth of influence. The neo-gothic style prompted a revival of the art of stained glass and coloured glass panels remained popular throughout the century. Living rooms were often now sited on the ground floor, stressing the connection with the outside world, and the English adopted French windows – pairs of glazed doors which opened out onto a balcony or garden.

But even such a diversity of influences pales alongside the stylistic vicissitudes of the Victorian era. Architects liked to show off as varied a set of references and sources as it was possible to find. Window shapes expressed every conceivable fashion; particularly popular were rounded, arched Italian windows, pointed neo-gothic types, stained glass and the angled bay, usually located at ground level or extending through two storeys.

The burgeoning industrial economy increased the demand for glass; improvements in technology meant that it could be made more cheaply. In the 1840s the excise tax on glass was repealed and in 1851 the Window Tax was abolished. Despite the resulting availability of glass, the Victorians had an ambivalent attitude to light. It was seen as a prerequisite for healthy working conditions, yet was all but excluded from domestic interiors.

The Pre-Raphaelite artists of the late nineteenth century had a passion for mediaeval decoration, and in particular for stained glass, which lent an ecclesiastic flavour to their highly moral work. Harmony *by Frank Dicksee (1853–1929) shows a romanticized interpretation of a domestic interior, its dramatic stained glass window partly shaded by a carmine red half curtain.*

Advances in iron and steel construction did, however, inspire new uses for glass and new types of windows. The glass roof and the conservatory were two Victorian innovations and great excitement was stimulated by the Crystal Palace, designed by Sir Joseph Paxton (1801–1865), which opened in 1851.

Twentieth-century Developments

By the late nineteenth century, new artistic ideas were developing. As well as a fascination for mediaeval 'honesty' and simple, early forms, which was advocated by the Arts and Crafts Movement, there was also a revival of 'Queen Anne'. Windows in this style were long and narrow and plainer in effect with panels fixed in lead or wooden glazing bars painted white, echoing an earlier era.

The sinuous, organic forms of Art Nouveau in the early years of the twentieth century also influenced window design. Expressive 'natural' shapes were made possible by the availability of cheap plate glass in the late nineteenth century and the development of the steel window frame.

Modern technology has enabled architects to design houses with window walls. The Glass House by Philip Johnson (1949) blends in with its landscape setting. Plate glass runs from floor to ceiling – perhaps the ultimate in window design.

The twentieth century has seen the window finally become independent of a building's structure. The architects of the Modern Movement used windows as a means of punctuating the solid mass of their designs, creating an interplay of solids and voids. After the Second World War, windows of any shape, size and configuration became possible. Steel beams could now span great distances unsupported and the wall became a mere infill rather than a structural component.

In 1949 the American architect, Philip Johnson (b. 1906), built his Glass House in New Canaan, Connecticut, where the windows *were* the walls. Large sheets of plate glass ran from ceiling to ground, dissolving the distinction between the inside and outside. Since then, further technological advances have seen entire buildings clad in glass – suspended glass walls hung like a curtain from the top.

Such developments have had a limited effect on domestic buildings. Today's new houses, often designed in imitation of past styles, incorporate a wide range of window sizes and shapes – from picture windows and arches to small, narrow lights. Window shapes are today as varied as the range of window treatments it is possible to create.

Window Styling

WINDOW STYLING

The window is a natural focal point in a room and the nature of the window itself – its shape, size, position and the modelling of its frame – lends character to the internal architecture. The window also has an important part to play in interior decoration. How it is treated – with curtains, blinds, valances and trimmings, in which colour and which fabric – affects the character and style of any room. Every window has enormous and exciting decorative potential.

Light

One of the most important ways in which window treatments influence the mood of a room is also one which is often least considered. Windows are designed to let in light. Natural light is not uniform in colour or intensity but dependent on a number of variables. The climate and directional aspect of a window have a bearing on the strength of the light while the season, time of day and weather are more local permutations. This inherent changeability gives life to any room, revealing the texture of interior surfaces, intensifying colours, casting transient shadows and enhancing architectural form through contrasts of light and shade.

The history of windows and window treatments is, in many ways, the story of light in the interior. In the Regency period, for example, it was commonplace for windows to be left uncovered, sometimes even undraped, and the sunlight to stream in untrammelled. Late Victorians, on the other hand, existed in semi-darkened rooms, the light filtered and screened to an inordinate degree. Fashion, rather than practicality, has dictated many of these variations.

Every option is open to us now. Most people enjoy natural light and for many city dwellers it is important to let in as much as the windows allow, as a subtle, changeable reminder of the natural world. Blinds or curtains need to be fixed back off the window when this is the case.

But for various reasons, including the protection of furniture from harsh sunlight or simply for the interesting effects it is possible to achieve, covering a window can be preferable. Depending on the fabric and style of covering, light is filtered to some degree. This offers the opportunity to enhance the quality of light, create patterns, evoke an atmosphere or even alter colours. Lace, printed voile or fine, unlined fabrics like muslin let in light but cast moody textural shadows. Half-drawn blinds generate drama by blocking and angling the light with the effect of a sunrise or sunset. An exaggerated swagged valance or draped pole casts a crescent-shaped shadow across a room when the sun is low behind it. Coloured fabrics act like stained glass, tinting the light and altering colours in the interior. A coloured or patterned *lining* can also create a range of subtle effects. Neutral linings in white or cream have become standard practice today, but past precedents reveal the use of soft colours and patterns for linings, which can warm up a cold room or brighten a dark one.

PREVIOUS PAGES *The rich, dull sheen of cotton sateen looks superbly sumptuous drawn up in billowing folds by a silky tasselled cord.*

LEFT *The warm yellow tones of this elegant drawing-room perfectly harmonize with the rich, golden glow of the afternoon sun that slants in through the French windows. The swagged valance casts its crescent-shaped shadow across the fireplace wall.*

BELOW *The transluscent quality of a simple, unlined window treatment can be used to colour an interior and create a particular mood. A plain roller blind in sapphire blue creates an atmosphere of cool tranquillity.*

Few rooms can boast quite such a fine prospect as this magnificent view over St James's Park to Westminster Abbey, depicted here by the French painter Louis Pierre Spindler. Plain curtains of muted brown velvet are softly caught back to frame the view, while the plain roller blind can be pulled right up out of the way. Tubs of geraniums link the inside and outside worlds, and soften the grandeur of the architecture.

Views

The window acts as a picture frame to the world beyond. But for every room with a view of the sea or rolling hills, there is at least one that overlooks a back yard, brick wall or neighbour's bathroom. It is important to utilize different styles of window treatment to either emphasize or alter what is revealed.

A really fine vista – Sydney Harbour or San Francisco Bay, heather-covered Scottish hills, perhaps – can either be left alone to stand for itself or emphasized with a frame of curtains or drapery. A plain, tailored window dressing – perhaps a box valance with neatly gathered curtains falling vertically to the floor – is probably most suitable, as it will not detract or compete in any way. However, a grander room may demand a more dramatic treatment, with a gently swagged valance and tie-backs to give the impression of old-fashioned theatre curtains.

If the view is not desirable, elaborate drapery combined with a half-drawn blind can replace it, providing a focal point in itself. When natural light is required but the view needs to be obscured, lace curtains or muslin provide effective coverings that create interesting effects too.

Scale and Proportion

The way a window is treated goes a long way towards either enhancing or helping to correct the basic proportions of a room. The length of a curtain or blind, its breadth and the use of decorative features such as valances, can all have an effect on the perception of space and the relation of one feature to another. On the grandest scale, if a stately dining-room has six long sash windows along one wall and each is decorated with glorious drapery in a strong colour falling to the floor, the length of the room will be emphasized by the effect of the vertical lines of the drapery. On the smallest scale, a cottage casement window will look even smaller if heavy curtains cover part of the window even when drawn back.

Few of us enjoy the luxury of wondering how best to utilize the size of palatial rooms. However, for every window and every room there are many permutations and the same rules apply. To lessen the impression of height, emphasize the horizontals; to lessen the width, emphasize the verticals. A very wide window with strong horizontal emphasis can be squared up by the use of narrow curtains extending down to the floor. In the same way, full and billowing drapery drawn either side of a window can widen a narrow shape.

Valances, too, can be used to change proportions. Many windows do not extend right to the cornice or ceiling and leave a spare margin of wall known as the 'dead light'. A valance that covers the dead light will have the effect of increasing the height of a room, whereas, when windows seem too tall, a valance hung below the top of the frame will reduce their stature. A further way is to attach a blind behind the valance or curtain and draw it down to cover part of the window. By releasing it or pulling it up again, the sense of height is restored.

The size and scale of a print have a bearing on proportion too. A large-scale

The intimate charm of a lowered festoon.

A wide, bright, airy look.

The slender silhouette of Regency style.

The elegant formality of tall curtains.

Well thought-out window treatments can create a powerful optical illusion that compensates for mean or ill-proportioned windows, even seeming to alter the architectural dimensions of a room to complement the chosen style of decoration. The effectiveness of the illusion is shown by four very different curtain designs for what is in fact the very same window.

23

LEFT *French windows open onto the Mediterranean in this French living room. White painted louvred shutters filter the brilliant sunlight; the cool blue stripes of simple, unlined curtains emphasize the smart, modern look of the room, while splashes of yellow add a touch of warmth and create a summery atmosphere.*

RIGHT *Many Laura Ashley fabric prints are inspired by antique originals gleaned from country-house sales, auctions and collections around the world. 'Blue Ribbons', the Laura Ashley design used for these curtains (top), was faithfully reproduced from a fragment of printed linen (centre) — a co-ordinating print of the rose motif was used for the wallpaper. The 'Country Lattice' design (below) was taken from an early nineteenth-century valance, reproduced on a fresh white background.*

floral design covering a small window might look out of proportion, while a tiny sprig or small-scale geometric pattern can be lost in grand curtains with generous pleats and swags unless they are boldly fringed or bordered.

Colour

Colour has always been a positive and powerful element in design. Those who imagine the rooms of the past were decorated in faded, delicate shades should look closely at contemporary pictures and reconstructions in museums and stately homes to see just how exuberant and theatrical many historical colour schemes were.

In many rooms, the window treatment forms an appreciable proportion of the surface area and the colour or colours it displays are therefore a vital part of a room's decorative scheme. There are no rules, merely traditions. At the most basic level, our response to different colours probably stems from colour in the natural world: reds, yellows and oranges are 'warm' because they suggest fire; greys and blues are 'cold' because they are the colours of water, ice, and clouds; greens and browns are comfortable because they are earth colours. These basic associations have given rise to some simple guidelines. To maximize light in a dull, sunless room, use spring-like yellows or pinks in the curtains and on the walls; to draw in a large empty area use the richer, darker shades of plum, burgundy and sage and a heavy window treatment to create a warmer, cosier feel; to promote cool restfulness in a bedroom use tones of blue and white.

This analysis is not, however, quite as straightforward as it seems. Centuries of cultural associations have given specific shades, such as Gustavian grey, Williamsburg blue and Federal green, their own nuances, which may transcend tonal values. Also, colours work together in surprising ways. A saffron yellow next to a royal blue may not look particularly strong, but next to cream its hue almost visibly changes.

Speaking very broadly, there are three ways of constructing a colour scheme. The easiest is to combine different tones of the same colour, decorating a room in a variety of greens, for example. The curtains could be made up in a strong jade damask with a darker fringe for emphasis, and upholstery in a green and pink print with walls in a pale ivory and light green stripe. Or complementary colours (yellow and blue, green and red, purple and orange) can be set against one another, perhaps with a mediating shade: thus red and green with brown, or yellow and blue with a touch of emerald. Often these colours occur together in fabric prints anyway and a particular colour from the print can be picked out and used on its own somewhere else. The most difficult, but perhaps the most effective, way is to assemble a palette of related shades – rose and candy pinks, say – and then inject a contrasting accent – sapphire – to strengthen them and bring them all to life.

Because colour is so powerful, people tend to play safe or use it in a purely remedial way, but to do this is to miss out on the excitement and vitality that colour can create. The foundation for most successful interiors is a confident and stylish use of colour, gained through experiment.

Print

Bringing rhythm and vitality to the interior, the use of print in decoration is an important consideration. Fabric prints – whether floral, geometric or figurative – synthesize colours, shapes, and even textures in a way that can create a mood or evoke a particular period, or is simply pleasing.

Modern manufacturing techniques mean that today we are in the privileged position of being able to choose from a wider variety of printed fabrics than ever before. Excellent reprints of traditional patterns are available – old chintzes and Victorian paisleys along with patterns from original woven fabrics.

As in other areas of interior decoration, using prints does not depend on strict adherence to a set of rules, but on a genuine appreciation for the effects they can create, and a sense of appropriateness regarding the style of the building and the function of the room. For a traditional country house look in a sitting room, a large-scale floral chintz immediately gives the desired effect, while a 'rustic' style can be achieved by hanging simple curtains showing a sprigged motif. Similarly, certain types of dark heavy damask with a textural design are high Victorian in style and very different from Chinese-inspired prints displaying motifs from oriental paintings or ceramics that give a colourful and exotic atmosphere.

It is always appropriate to match the print to the period of the house. It is difficult to find many fabrics displaying designs used in Elizabethan or Jacobean

ABOVE *Plain fabrics or geometrical prints are not the only choices for a modern interior. The strict minimalism of this apartment is softened by the use of a Duncan Grant print for the curtains, lending a Bohemian touch. Muted shades of grey and yellow marry the two styles perfectly.*

LEFT *A floral chintz – almost synonymous with English country house style – is traditional yet fresh, comfortable yet crisp, and the ideal choice for a country drawing-room.*

textiles, but fabrics using prints from the eighteenth century onwards are now widely available. These copies are not restricted to English print sources, but draw on old French and Italian designs too.

It is important to consider the room as a whole, not just the curtains or blinds in isolation. You may find that all the pattern you need in a particular room can be supplied by a window treatment; otherwise, perhaps in a very large room, you may want to coordinate curtains and upholstery or even create a densely layered effect, with sympathetic prints used together on different surfaces.

Different prints work together in several ways. They may show some affinity, having been specifically designed to complement each other, sharing a common motif, perhaps on a different scale, or colour. Or they may contrast in a definite but pleasing way. It can be very effective to set off curtains in a blue and yellow lattice print with a yellow and white striped roller blind, or curtains in a Chinoiserie floral print with a blind in a Chinese-inspired fretwork design.

Texture

The great furnishing fabrics of the past — damask, velvet, brocade and chintz — evoke a sense of luxury and comfort that is partly to do with their textural qualities. The first three, especially, are gorgeous to feel as well as to look at; their weight and thickness inspire visions of rich, elaborate curtains and bed-hangings in the great houses of the wealthy in centuries past. These fabrics are still available today and, with the right choice and combination of fabrics, window treatments can create a mood of period opulence.

ABOVE *The dormer window of a quintessential cottage bedroom is decorated with simple sill-length curtains in a rustic sprig pattern. Small repeat patterns in soft, muted shades are timelessly charming in such a setting.*

LEFT *The art of combining patterns is seen by the window of a morning-room. Two further patterns have been chosen to work well with the curtain material, linked by a common colour scheme.*

ABOVE *The texture of fabric is a key aspect of successful window treatments, and different fabrics lend their own particular qualities to a design. A crisp cotton chintz makes an elegant statement in a formal drawing-room, caught back by a brass rosette boss.*

LEFT *An ivory cotton damask print complements delicate voile undercurtains, set off by the exposed brick of the window reveal.*

Other textures promote different moods. Plain cotton is crisp and fresh-looking; linen union has a matt, textured look; glazed chintz has a reflective sheen; silk is soft and rich and also reflects the light. These textures can be utilized to reinforce the impressions already prevalent in a room while texture itself can be enhanced by the use of trimmings in a contrasting material. A cotton block fringe on glazed chintz or gold braid on velvet will set off the main fabric.

Textural interest can be further emphasized by the actual style of the window treatment. A plain box valance over pleated cotton curtains produces a neat, tailored look in keeping with the crispness of the material, while looped and draped swags and tails exploit the richness of velvet. A softly gathered heading suits the delicacy of lace and a ruched blind makes the most of the reflective surface of glazed chintz.

Texture is an evocative aspect of interior design that is too often disregarded. The right texture can make all the difference to the success of a window treatment.

Period

There is a strong historical precedent for reintroducing designs from the past. Often, what we like to categorize as a particular period style is itself full of references to earlier sources: Regency style derived much of its inspiration from classical Greece and ancient Egypt; the late Victorians were fascinated by Japanese decoration and the Edwardians enjoyed a vogue for the sedate sensibilities of Queen Anne. Then as now, changing fashions did not necessarily demand that interiors were completely refurnished, and furniture and fabrics from earlier times often co-existed happily beside the new.

There are two ways of recreating a period style. One is to assess the character and origins of your house and carefully reproduce furnishings, colours and details of precisely the right period, scale and grandeur. Devotees of this approach take great pains to ensure that everything is authentic, from the finials on the curtain poles to the fabric design. The other approach is more eclectic, assembling a variety of ideas which are sympathetic to one another and which work together to generate a particular atmosphere.

John Fowler (1906–77), the great twentieth-century English decorator, had a great respect for the rich variety of historical styles and, while his traditional interiors were precise in their references, he often combined different elements with imagination and flair. He found the curtain treatments of the past were a fascinating source for ideas, and adopted a selection of elegant styles.

Although curtains did not become an established decorative feature in the interior until the seventeenth century, since then there has been an immense variety of styles. From the tasselled festoon curtains of the early Georgians, to the romantic, draped confections of French Empire style, the pretty swags, trimmed with rosettes and bows, of the Regency period, and the fringed valances, dress curtains and swathes of lace of high Victoriana, the precedents have been set for window treatments to suit any period house.

John Fowler was one of the most influential and admired decorators of the century. A master of detail and a devotee of pre-Victorian styles, he is well-known for his innovative window treatments, many of which were combinations of different period elements rather than strictly accurate reproductions. This staircase window in a farmhouse he decorated in 1939–40 shows some characteristic touches in the Empire style: a draped valance, rosettes, tasselled cords and a contrasting pinked frill. Behind the scalloped valance, a roller blind has been painted trompe l'oeil *to look like slatted wood.*

Curtains

CURTAINS

'Curtains' is a generic name with, perhaps, an old-fashioned resonance for what is now a very wide variety of fabric window decorations. The word may more immediately evoke the most common and simple style with gathered or pleated fabric falling straight down from a track or rod, but it also describes exuberant swagged and tailed drapery.

Curtains play a major role in the decoration of all kinds of interiors. They add colour, texture or pattern (or all three) to a scheme, soften or emphasize the architectural qualities of the room or the window itself, and provide a pleasing sense of warmth and intimacy. They can also be very dramatic, and provide a focal point in a room. Practically, they screen or filter light, provide privacy at night and insulate against noise or draughts.

For these reasons, it is easy to imagine that curtains would have been one of the principal features of the earliest interiors. Yet, surprisingly, they are a comparatively recent phenomenon, only coming into their own in the late seventeenth century. From this point onwards, they quickly became established as an important aspect of furnishing, reflecting and expressing a wealth of stylistic changes in the succeeding centuries.

The Development of Curtains

Perhaps because early window openings were rarely large enough to cause significant heat loss, curtains did not evolve primarily as a means of insulation. In mediaeval times and up to the seventeenth century, wall- and bed-hangings, often made from richly woven or embroidered tapestries, served this function. Neither did curtains exist to provide privacy. In early houses, with rooms opening directly off one another and beds often placed in reception rooms, there was little privacy anyway. At night shutters made the windows secure.

The style of the first curtains indicates that their function was to filter light: they were usually made of a single length of thin, unlined material, such as linen or silk and hung at one side of the window from iron rings on an iron rod. When necessary this single curtain would be drawn across the window by hand or by a length of cord. Although, by the seventeenth century, a room might display richly coloured and patterned textiles – wall-hangings, bed-curtains with valances and table-carpets – the curtains usually had no decorative purpose. Often, perhaps where light was at a premium, windows were left uncovered.

The emergence of decorative curtains coincided with the development of the sash window at the end of the seventeenth century. Windows no longer opened inwards; they became larger and more graceful-looking with lighter frames. To set off this new architectural feature, curtains assumed a more important, flamboyant role. First of all, they were divided to create a symmetrical pair. Then the bare arrangement of rod and rings was covered with a valance. To give unity, these new curtains were usually made of the same material as the wall- and bed-

PRECEDING PAGES *The large metal-framed windows in the living-room of a converted warehouse have been formally dressed with two layers of curtains: ivory cotton damask-print outer curtains and filmy voile cross-over drapery. With the curtains pulled back well clear of the window frame, the windows look even larger, while the billowing voile softly filters the light.*

BELOW *This seventeenth-century Dutch interior, painted by Cornelius Janssens (1593–1661) and entitled* The Sweeper, *shows an early type of curtain – a single unlined hanging on plain rings which drew to one side of the window by means of a cord. The curtains coordinate with the chair upholstery both in colour and type of fabric.*

hangings – silk damask, velvet or worsted – but there were thinner, lighter curtains as well, in taffeta, gauze or silk.

Soon after, at the beginning of the eighteenth century, early Georgian decorators introduced the first 'festoon' hangings. Single curtains that drew up in soft billows to a valance-covered board – and often left hanging well below the top of the window these rapidly became the fashion in both town and country.

From the late eighteenth century through to the early decades of the nineteenth, curtain style went through a number of changes in Europe. Before the French Revolution of 1789, Parisian upholsterers in particular exhibited a high degree of skill, creating extremely elaborate drapery, combining different fabrics and using trimmings lavishly. Asymmetry was particularly fashionable. Later, when Napoleon was enthroned, great lengths of luxurious fabric were artfully thrown over poles to fall in extravagant pleats to the floor; they introduced a note of disorder and romance into Empire interiors and softened the severe lines of the furniture. The effect was emphasized by the use of gauzy materials such as silk and muslin. Stripes were also popular, as was satin in clear, strong colours.

After 1800, divided curtains became popular again in England. Rods and rings became much more decorative and obvious, with elaborate brackets and finials, fixed hold-backs (*embrasses*) and cleats. Undercurtains in contrast fabrics were common. Plainer treatments also enjoyed a certain vogue and many windows were not curtained at all but merely had a festooned valance to soften the lines of the frame or accentuate the rounded outline of an arch.

Two (or more) identical windows side by side often at this time inspired 'continued drapery', in which the whole wall was treated as a single composition,

ABOVE *In the late eighteenth and early nineteenth centuries, 'continued drapery' was a fashionable scheme in which the entire wall was treated as a single unit. This illustration of 1838 shows three windows united by a single valance.*

This mid-Victorian interior, the dressing-room of Alexandra, daughter of Czar Nicholas I, at Schloss Fasanerie near Fulda in Germany, shows how elaborate window treatments became during the nineteenth century. There are three layers of curtain at this window – a muslin undercurtain just visible beneath the dressing-table, lace curtains and heavy outer curtains matching the deep draped valance above.

the design of one window perhaps matching the other asymmetrically. A coloured curtain (designed to cover the whole window when released) might be tied back to the left and its white undercurtain tied back to the right to give a two-colour daytime effect, while the second window would be dressed in reverse. As a pair they would match in mirror-image.

The early Victorian period saw the arrival of the *lambrequin*, a flat, shaped valance which framed the top of the window and descended almost to the floor on either side, cutting out a great deal of light. This was often combined with both outer and inner curtains for a full, layered effect. A plainer treatment consisted of a pair of curtains suspended from a decorative pole and tied back low down. Curtains were heavy and dark, often trailing on the floor. Contrasting linings might be turned over the leading edges to make interesting borders.

The stuffy, overpoweringly upholstered look associated with the Victorian interior only took hold in the last few decades of the nineteenth century. The intention seemed to have been to exclude as much light as possible. Many reasons have been given to explain the fashion for gloom. One idea is that it was a question of prestige: if a man's family could exist in darkness it proved they did not need to lift a finger for themselves. Window coverings also created a slightly mysterious atmosphere.

A typical window arrangement in this style might consist of a valance, main curtains, inner lace curtains, perhaps crossed-over, and short 'glass curtains' made of muslin or net set against the lower panes of the window. All would be tasselled, fringed and corded. There were even treatments where drapery covered drapery, suspended from a second pole above the main one.

Naturally enough, reaction soon set in. The end of the nineteenth century was a time of stylistic re-evaluation. The Arts and Crafts Movement and the beginnings of the Modern Movement (which would make a real impact after the First World War) combined to simplify and lighten window treatments generally, editing out superfluous decoration and essentially forming the foundation for twentieth-century taste.

The Queen Anne revival led directly to what we now recognize as the English country house style – a comfortable, informed and pretty look that derives from no one particular period but manages to combine elements of Georgian, Regency and Victorian taste. This approach to decoration relies heavily on traditional window treatments, with simple but decorative valances and divided curtains, using fabrics such as floral chintz.

At the other extreme, the influence of the Modern Movement in design and architecture led to pared-down, forthright, 'clean' interiors, with curtains playing a minor, more utilitarian role. Between these two broad approaches, there have been more specific period revivals: neo-Georgian between the wars and again in the 1980s; Regency in the 1930s and immediately post-war; and a reappraisal of Victoriana in the 1970s.

Cottage or rustic style has also become increasingly popular in the last thirty years and many town and city dwellers have adopted the style in high-rise flats and terraced houses as a substitute for the dream of a country home. This idealized cottage style does not really resemble the humble households of the past; much of what we assume in the way of window decoration, upholstery and accoutrements is based on a prettified myth.

In the twentieth century the style demands the use of strong, plain fabrics such as cotton and linen – perhaps displaying a sprigged or old-fashioned floral print – for curtains, hung from rods of bare wood. Lace is often used decoratively for borders or undercurtains, as well as tablecloths and valances on mantelpieces.

The frequency of modern revivals, a result of improved manufacturing techniques and communications, is unique to the twentieth century but the diversity of style is nothing new. Ideas about decoration have been borrowed, reinterpreted and revived through the centuries.

The little casement window of a pretty cottage bedroom is hung with simple curtains and valance of plain cream calico. Seclusion by Edmund Blair Leighton (1853–1922) shows the early twentieth-century version of the perennially popular rustic style of decoration, which stood in marked contrast both to the heavy pomp of the mainstream Victorian decorative style and to the rarified aestheticism of Art Nouveau.

The simplicity of this single curtain in muslin, suspended from a narrow brass rod, makes an evocative contrast with the dark panelled surfaces and rich upholstery of this period interior.

Curtain Styles

Fabric

The enormous variety of fabrics now available makes any curtain effect possible. When considering different fabrics, always bear in mind the effect you are trying to achieve.

The most luxurious fibre is silk, woven from threads extracted from the cocoons of silkworms. It is available in a variety of textures – all of which can be exploited in different ways. Light, transparent organza has a translucence suited to delicate, feminine treatments; textured raw or slub silk can be used in more formal environments and looks superb in dining- or sitting-rooms, its colours reflected in glass or silver; glossy, sumptuous silk taffeta deserves an extravagant curtain design in the grand manner to show off its opulence; rich velvets are warm and well suited to cosier rooms – although of course they look regal in any setting. All silks drape well and were the preferred fabrics of the Georgians, especially the silk brocades and damasks.

Since the late eighteenth century, when printed cottons and muslins became popular and the French silk industry went into decline, silk has really been a luxury. However, the quality and variety of modern cottons and linens is such that they provide a popular substitute, especially as some are now printed with old silk designs. Cotton is strong and hardwearing and prints well. This particular ability to take clear, bright colours has made cotton the mainstay of soft furnishing since the nineteenth century.

The crisp, classic look of plain-weave cotton furnishing fabric makes it suitable for a wide range of window treatments – everything from gingham café curtains to formal swagged and tailed curtains in a rich paisley print. The lightweight even-weave cotton known as muslin has a matt, filmy texture which makes it particularly useful for romantic, draped effects. Chintz, the traditional English furnishing fabric originally produced in India, has a glazed finish which gives it an exceptional combination of lustre and crispness. Cotton sateen, a heavyweight cotton with a satin weave, makes soft, luxurious drapery and was much used in late Victorian drawing-rooms. Cotton is also the basis for many velvets.

Linen, which is derived from the flax plant, is another natural fibre available in various weights and weaves – from fine, soft lawn to the sturdier linen union. Linen or linen/cotton blends are sometimes used in damask, a rich woven fabric with a raised pattern that is perfect for recreating Georgian curtain styles.

BELOW *A classic damask, copied from an original eighteenth-century design, creates an effect of gracious splendour in this Georgian dining-room. The subtleties of the blue tones are set off by a flamboyant rose-pink lining and fringe.*

LEFT *Floral chintz adds depth and distinction to this country house drawing-room. The particular fresh quality of this fabric stems from its glazed finish, which produces a reflective sheen.*

Lightweight, unlined curtains are an attractive option for warm, sunny climates, filtering rather than blocking the light. The sapphire stripes of these unlined chintz curtains tint the intense light of the Florida sun, flooding this dining room with a cool blue hue.

A window covering that is often ignored today is a hanging carpet or rug. Just as, in previous centuries, woven tapestries and carpets were used to block draughts in a decorative way, so carpets and rugs in rich colours can now be hung on poles to luxurious effect.

Lining and interlining

The practical advantages of lining curtains are well known. Lining protects curtains from fading, makes them wear longer, increases insulation and reduces noise. A lined curtain also has a professional look; it hangs better and keeps its shape.

More importantly, lining can also fulfil more decorative functions, an aspect widely appreciated in previous eras. From the early nineteenth century onwards, curtains were often lined in a colour or contrasting pattern, sometimes with the lining turned over the leading edge of the fabric to provide a decorative border. Only in the last few decades of this century have linings tended to be restricted to plain white, off-white or cream, probably for reasons of economy.

Just as unlined, semi-transparent curtains can diffuse the light, a coloured lining can act as a filter. A pink lining combined with a translucent curtain can add a subtle, warming tint to the light which shines through it. Yellow lining can make a room seem sunny and cheerful, even on a grey morning.

Patterned or contrast-coloured linings can generate a great deal of interest even where the curtains are more or less opaque. The lining can display a motif, perhaps on a smaller scale, taken from the curtain material, or it can pick up one of the colours. Curtains can be caught back to reveal the lining and the colour echoed in trimmings or tie-backs. A particular attraction is the way the curtains look from outside: coloured or patterned linings give an interesting and welcoming aspect to the exterior.

The highest degree of quality, however, can be achieved by not just lining but interlining too. Interlining consists of adding a layer of blanketing fabric between the curtain and lining, increasing insulation and effectively blocking light. The principle advantage of interlining is that it acts like a layer of padding, creating heavy, rounded folds. It makes even the finest cotton hang better, lending both weight and texture.

Headings

Choosing a heading is rather like choosing the style of a dress. Practicalities aside, the heading will determine whether the curtain is formal and tailored, soft and flowing, simple or sophisticated. If the heading is intended to be seen, not covered with a valance or drapery, it acquires even more importance.

Formal treatments that are well suited to display include pencil pleats, box pleats, triple pleats, goblet pleats and French pleats. These tailored headings are all interesting in themselves. They are fairly deep and keep the fabric hanging in full, straight folds.

Softer effects can be achieved by standard gathering. This is a shallow

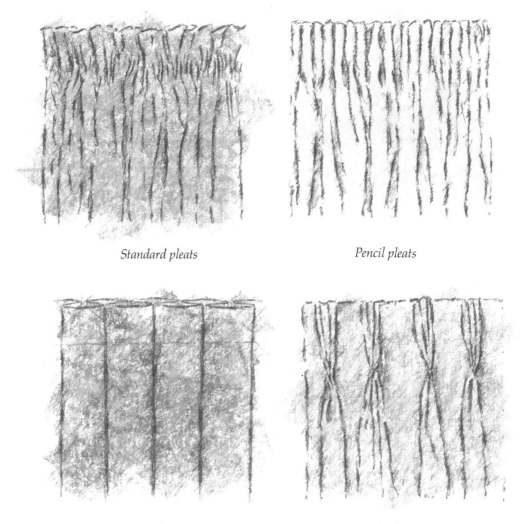

Standard pleats

Pencil pleats

Box pleats

Triple pleats

The curtain heading will set the style of the overall effect. Simple gathered headings give an informal, cottagey effect; pencil pleats have a neater, crisper look, while box pleats are a bold, structured heading to complement a smart, formal interior. Triple pleats in all their varieties offer an elegant solution that will enhance a more formal decorative scheme.

OVERLEAF There is an equally wide variety of headings for curtains that hang from poles — from the simple elegance of triple pleats and rings or the softer, gathered look of a cased heading to the briskly practical fabric loops, or the pretty frivolity of bows.

French pleats

Goblet pleats

Fabric loops with pole

Fabric bows with pole

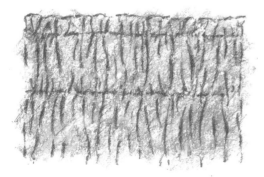

Triple pleats with rings

Cased heading with pole

heading that works well combined with valances. Alternatively, a stand-up curtain top can be created using a cased heading: this involves inserting a pole through a gathered tunnel set a few inches from the top of the curtain.

Certain heading styles suit particular patterns and textures. The crispness of pencil pleats can be emphasized by a striped fabric, while rich, textured cloth works well with a goblet heading. A trellis pattern can be very effective with a smocked heading. Short, lightweight curtains, including café curtains (which only cover the bottom half of a window) and lace panels, can be hung by means of a cased heading. The fabric gathers along the rod, creating a pretty shirring.

Simple but highly decorative treatments can be created by making a feature of the means of suspension. These informal effects use soft ties, feminine bows or wide loops in the fabric of the curtain, or a toning or contrasting fabric, to attach the curtain to a pole or rod in the place of heading tape and hooks. The curtain top can be scalloped to give additional interest.

Lengths, widths and shapes

The dimensions of a curtain are as much a question of style as practicality. The length and breadth of any window treatment can have an important effect on our perception of a room's proportions and the proportion of the window itself, and can also emphasize particular qualities of fabric and the style of dressing. The print or design will have a bearing on the proportions also. A pattern with a strong vertical emphasis will heighten a room. A pattern with a large-scale motif generally needs a large area to work well and gain the benefit of the repeat.

The fullness of a curtain depends on the type of heading, and different headings require different amounts of material. Standard gathering, for example, can be successfully accomplished using the minimum: a width of fabric one and a half times the length of the pole or track. Pencil pleats, however, demand a width of two and a half times. It is always better to err on the side of generosity as narrow, skimpy curtains will never hang properly and may even fail to meet at the centre.

The width of the pole or track will be determined by the type and size of window and the amount of light you want to let in when the curtains are pulled back. The length of the curtains can be varied, according to the mood and style you wish to create. In general, most curtains either hang to the sill or the floor. Sill-length curtains are inevitably more informal and countrified than floor-length ones, which suggest a grander setting, and are often needed for practical reasons in kitchens or bathrooms. They are also the best answer for very wide windows or those placed high in a wall, situations where floor-length curtains would look out of proportion.

Within the concept of sill and floor lengths, however, there are certain subtleties. Sill-length curtains can just touch the sill or can more extravagantly cover it; similarly, floor-length hangings can finish just above the floor, rest on it or even drape it. This last effect can look both luxurious and romantic, and it is a style which is just as successful in a lightweight fabric such as muslin as it is in velvet. The fabric can be flared, fanned out like the base of a column or tumbled on the floor in rich folds.

FAR LEFT *Curtains look particularly luxurious if they are allowed to drape on to the floor instead of clearing it. In this formal dining-room, elegant windows are hung with a ribbon-patterned fabric, caught back low down and fluted out at the base in a gentle curve.*

LEFT *Sill-length curtains create a more casual look for a modern living room, but still look sophisticated if taken down just below the sill.*

ABOVE *A kitchen demands a practical curtain treatment, and sill-length curtains in a simple liquorice-striped cotton have a crisp, fresh look that is entirely appropriate.*

ABOVE *The height at which a curtain is tied back affects its shape and overall style. For a landing window, where only a certain amount of light is required, a full single curtain is loosely tied at the half-way point, allowing the fabric print to be displayed.*

ABOVE RIGHT *An enchanting period look can be achieved by tying drapery back high up with decorative* embrasses, *creating a stylish Empire line.*

FAR RIGHT *For tall windows in a large room, curtains joined at the top and softly drawn back very low down emphasize the verticals and thus the height and scale of the room.*

Another important consideration is whether the curtains are to be tied back or left to hang straight. They can be tied back either by cording them at the appropriate height and pulling them up diagonally to resemble very loose, centrally divided swags and tails, or by using tie-backs. The height at which these are placed will partly determine the style of the window treatment. Regency curtains were tied back very low, or very high, sometimes both. Victorian tie-backs were often placed quite low and were an important aspect of curtain design because without them the curtains would simply swing shut, being drawn together at the top.

Rods and poles

The first curtains were hung from plain iron rods but this basic arrangement soon gave way to highly decorative poles, held in place by elaborate brackets. In 1790, the 'French rod' was invented, a device which incorporated pulleys and cords and allowed curtains to be drawn from one side.

Versions of all these basic types are available today. Practical requirements – the weight of the curtains, type of heading, and so on – will largely dictate which style to adopt. Most rods and tracks are functional and designed to be covered

BELOW *Ornamental poles are intended for display. A simple wooden pole lends a country air when used with rustic sprig prints; an ornate brass pole with a pineapple finial, or capped with a flourish of Prince of Wales feathers, looks sumptuous used with rich, swagged hangings; alternatively, a fluted brass pole has a restrained elegance swathed in drapery, while an oak pole with an acorn finial has a dignified look when combined with heavy brocade.*

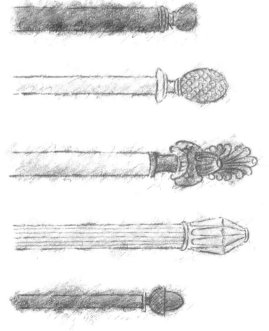

by the heading or valance; poles, on the other hand, are made for display.

Ornate fluted brass poles with decorative brackets and finials can add grandeur to period drapery; carved lion heads, pineapples and even acorns were popular motifs in the past and are faithfully reproduced on finials now. Plainer versions are elegant and formal and work well with the simpler curtain styles. Wooden poles offer the opportunity for a countrified look hung with rustic sprig prints or chintzes, but used to suspend heavy brocades, they assume a dignified and old-fashioned look. Varnishing enhances the richness of mahogany while staining brings out the patterns of the wood grain. Paint provides a variety of opportunities for colour coordination or contrast; poles in white paint can help to create the effects of the Regency period when combined with drapery in the ice-cream colours of vanilla, strawberry and pistachio. The poles can be swathed in drapery or used to suspend swagged hangings for theatrical effects.

Metal rods, lighter and narrower than poles, are designed for use with lightweight curtains, curtains with cased headings, café curtains and window treatments which need to hang close to the glass. On casement windows and French doors rods could be used to fix the curtains within each frame, so that they open with the window.

Blinds

BLINDS

The fabric blind is a versatile and popular form of window treatment. The simplest variety is the roller blind, which draws down flat over the window to make a neat and unobtrusive screen. Another classically plain style is the roman blind, which pleats horizontally. The third and most decorative form includes the festoon and the Austrian festoon, where a fullness of fabric is ruched and drawn up in soft, billowing, crescent-shaped folds. Used on their own or in conjunction with curtains or valances, these blinds can express a range of decorating styles.

Blinds have many practical advantages. They are an economic alternative to curtains since generally much less fabric is required to make them. They are often the best solution in kitchens or bathrooms, or wherever full-length curtains are not sensible, and can also be highly effective on awkwardly shaped or positioned windows which would otherwise be difficult to cover. Their prime function, however, is to screen light; in this respect they are particularly versatile as they can be lowered to control the amount of sunlight a room receives.

The Development of Blinds

In hot countries, blinds have been a common solution to the problem of screening strong light since the earliest times. As today, many of these were woven rush or split cane (canisse). In the West, however, interior shutters largely fulfilled this role until the early seventeenth century, when the 'sash' first made an appearance.

The 'sash' was a forerunner of today's sun blind. Often installed in living rooms to screen glare, it consisted of a wooden frame attached to the window, over which was stretched a piece of linen or silk. The fabric was often dyed green or another dark colour, and was sometimes oiled to make it translucent. (A green tint was thought to have a beneficial effect on the eyesight.)

Sashes remained popular throughout the eighteenth century, even persisting into Regency times. Occasionally they were hinged along one side so they could be easily swung back when needed. The fabric panel might also be pleated.

Festoon curtains – a new style of window covering and the forerunner of our festoon blinds – were widely adopted after 1720. The first festoons consisted of a single hanging which drew up in swags by means of cords and pulleys concealed behind the valance board. Many of these – made in silks and damasks – were used on their own, softening or adding drama to elegant Georgian windows.

The eighteenth century also saw a new invention – the roller blind. In 1741, an English tradesman advertised 'spring' blinds, promoting their advantages: 'Convenient to keep the Sun off in Summer'. Early rollers were often made of copper or brass and the blinds themselves could be highly decorative. Although in 1755 Madame de Pompadour's boudoir was described as being furnished with a taffeta roller blind, on which was painted garlands of flowers, such elaboration only became universally popular in the early nineteenth century. At that time,

A fringed roller blind is framed by a deep-cut tasselled pelmet in this French boudoir of 1840. The blind is painted with an elaborate Chinese-style scene, reflecting the prevailing taste for the exotic East.

PRECEDING PAGES *Blinds have great versatility as well as being practical. The simple roller blind has a neat, minimal look, the roman blind has a classic outline with its regular folds of fabric, while the festoon shows blinds at their most decorative with softly ruched swags that will complement any window.*

designs and decorative borders were painted in oils on silk, linen and wire gauze blinds. The fabric might also be varnished in places to allow light through.

From the middle of the nineteenth century, blinds became an indispensable part of many elaborate window treatments. Roller or holland blinds were the most fashionable variety and these were often elaborately printed, woven or painted. Edges were shaped or bordered with openwork and trimmed with fringes and tassels. It was common for blinds to display landscapes or other pastoral themes and some were painted to look like stained glass.

These effects were not always entirely successful. The showiness and poor execution of some decorated blinds promoted a return to plain varieties, either in neutral, natural tones or a solid colour. There was even a brief fashion for red holland blinds, which must have added a special note of richness to late Victorian interiors. Plain holland blinds, however, generally had a utilitarian look and served primarily as sun shades. An 1852 inventory of Clarence House, then the residence of the Duchess of Kent, mentions holland blinds as part of the furnishing of the attic rooms, used as a dormitory for domestic staff.

In the late nineteenth century, the festooned 'Austrian shade' became popular. A blind with a scalloped edge that retained its fully ruched appearance even when let down, it was used as a substitute for light undercurtains and was generally made of translucent material like net or even silk.

The simpler styles of the roman and roller blind have found a particular application in modern interiors, a use which has tended to emphasize their utilitarian qualities. But, in recent times, the reappearance of the festoon heralded the return of a more decorative approach. There remains great scope for achieving many different effects with blinds.

ABOVE *By the mid-nineteenth century, blinds were generally plainer than their elaborately painted predecessors. Often neutral in colour, they might be made of lace, or else prettily embellished with whitework or cutwork embroidery. John Atkinson Grimshaw's* Summer *of 1875 shows how these simple, delicately translucent blinds might be used on their own during the summer months.*

LEFT *The late-nineteenth-century vogue for handsome festoon shades is seen in* The Rivals *by James Tissot, where they frame the view into a luxuriantly planted conservatory.*

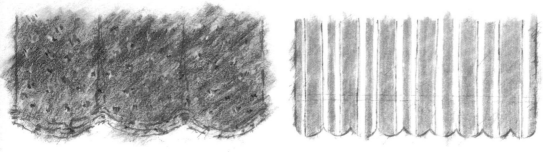

Plain festoon

Scallop-edged roller blind

LEFT *There is a style of blind to complement every decorative scheme. The simplest roller blind can be enlivened with shaped edges; a plain roman blind can be given a smart border, or crisp castellations; the fuller festoon blind can be left plain, or dressed up with frills and choux or frivolously ruffled pinking for an extravagant, sumptuous effect.*

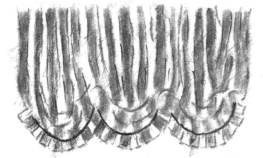

Half frilled festoon

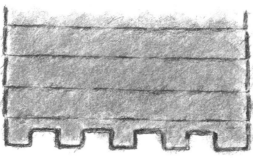

Serpentine roller blind

Fully frilled festoon with choux

Castellated roman blind

FAR RIGHT ABOVE *Roller blinds in sapphire blue make a smart statement in a bay window without detracting from the intricate pattern of leaded panes. Their translucent quality infuses the interior with a cool blue hue, creating a tranquil, contemplative mood.*

RIGHT ABOVE *Teamed with other window treatments, roller blinds offer an opportunity for colour co-ordination and contrast.*

RIGHT BELOW *Simple striped roller blinds are dressed up with a draped floral valance decoratively flung over a pole, in a successful blend of styles and prints.*

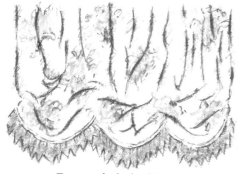

Deep-pinked edged festoon

Roman blind with contrast border

Blind Styles

Roller blinds

Simple, cheap and practical, the roller or holland blind has maintained its popularity ever since it was first introduced. Its crisp, neat appearance makes it particularly suitable for use on small windows and in modern settings. But it is also adaptable enough to work well in more traditional rooms, especially when given an elegant serpentine edge and combined with curtains or a valance. It can display a single block of colour, a coordinating or small-scale pattern, stripes or a large pictorial design.

Roller blinds are designed to cover the window and should not extend further than the frame. If the window is recessed, the blind can be hung so that it fits against the glass; otherwise, the blind can be mounted on the frame itself or on the wall immediately above.

Fabric which is specially stiffened for making into roller blinds is available in a wide range of colours and patterns. A neat white or cream holland blind may suit your requirements perfectly, but there is no need for such restraint. A small stylized or floral repeat pattern, coordinated with wallpaper, looks charming and fresh in a bedroom; stripes can look either elegant or informally cheerful, depending on their colour and setting; large, pictorial motifs are enjoyed by children. Except for the blackout variety, roller blinds do not block the light completely so even a plain colour will tint the light in an interesting way.

The most imaginative way to use roller blinds, however, is either to complement or contrast the colours, pattern and texture of the blinds with curtains or drapery. Yellow and white striped blinds set off a green and yellow floral chintz in a very pleasing way. Similarly, a dark red blind looks rich and

ABOVE *The crisp concertina folds of a roman blind fit neatly into the deep recess of a bathroom window. Roman blinds are particularly well-suited to small-scale repeat patterns.*

ABOVE RIGHT *On a larger scale, a splashy pastel floral print is a cheerful choice of fabric for a roman blind*

FAR RIGHT *Theatrical without being overwhelming, plain festoon blinds with a contrast banding and fringe underline the cool elegance of a formal drawing-room.*

warm behind a draped, spice-coloured paisley pelmet in a cosy study. Using a coloured blind behind lace drapery is effective because it emphasizes the patterns in the lace when drawn down.

Roman blinds

The classic lines of the roman blind give a room a sense of elegance and proportion. Neat without being severe, the roman blind pulls up into horizontal pleats that display fabric to advantage. Like the roller blind, the roman fits flat against the window and is an ideal window covering in situations where a full-length treatment would be impractical. But it also works very well teamed with curtains because its folds complement the pleats and folds of the drapery.

Choosing a fabric for roman blinds needs an element of care. Some patterns, particularly those displaying large floral or circular motifs, can look distinctly odd when pleated horizontally. Geometric prints, stripes and checks are a more sympathetic choice and can be chosen to complement plain or even floral curtains or valances. The most pleasing effects with roman blinds, however, are often not due to the print, but the texture. A fabric such as linen union that displays an obvious texture looks stylish and sets the tone of the room.

The tailored effect of this type of blind can be further emphasized by trimming — and these trimmings can be matched to curtains or other upholstery. A contrast lining turned back over the edges of the blind makes a neat border, while bands in braid or fabric can be inset to form panels. Scalloped edging would be at odds with the regular pleats of roman blinds, but a castellated edge is effective.

Deeply swagged festoons in a warm paisley print, trimmed with a bullion fringe, give a rich period look.

BELOW *A fresh, pretty blue and white bathroom is perfectly complemented by a simple festoon blind trimmed with a deep, blue frill.*

Austrian festoon blinds

Today, the Austrian festoon is enjoying a renewed popularity. Combining many of the practical advantages of a blind with the fuller effect of a curtain, this type of treatment can be used on its own to dress up a window – adding a touch of theatricality and resembling a valance when drawn up – or set between curtains for a really rich, draped effect. Depending entirely on the choice of fabric, heading and trimming, the Austrian festoon can look soft and sculptural, frilly and feminine, or grand and formal.

The Austrian festoon is often hung fairly low at the window, rather than pulled right up, so long sash windows are particularly well suited to this treatment. It is also possible to pull the centre of the blind higher than the edges, creating an arch of fabric and framing the view through the window. The generous billows of the festoon always look luxurious and recall the opulent treatments in silk and damask in eighteenth-century interiors.

Because the fabric is only softly gathered at the base of the blind, a wider range of patterns is suitable than in the case of roman blinds. Bold Regency stripes can look supremely elegant in a drawing-room; pretty floral designs emphasize a country house look in a bedroom or bathroom; a plain weave will bring out the sculptural effect of the ruching for a study or conservatory.

The choice of heading will partly determine the style of the Austrian festoon. For a full effect, with the blind looking similar to a gathered or pleated curtain when let down, choose one of the curtain headings: pencil pleats or box pleats, for example. Otherwise the blind can be given a cased heading and ruffled on a rod so that the top edge has a decorative shirring; this is a less formal effect. If the top of the blind is to be covered by a valance – this combination is very

The inherent romance of a conservatory is played up to the full with rose-covered festoons trimmed with bows to create a feminine bower.

suitable for a formal, even grand, reception room — then standard gathering is all that is needed. Alternatively, for a flatter effect, the top of the blind can be attached to a rail in the same way as a roman blind.

For Austrian festoon blinds made with curtain headings, the best materials to use are curtain fabrics such as cotton furnishing fabric, chintz, cotton sateen and linen union. All are crisp and sturdy enough to pleat up well. Lining greatly improves the shape of the folds and helps to screen light. Austrian festoon blinds with cased headings or simply attached to a rail like a roman blind can, however, be made in a lightweight fabric and left unlined so that the textural qualities of the material are enhanced and a shimmery light filters through.

Festoon blinds lend themselves naturally to being trimmed with frills, flounces and fringes. A deep frill of coordinating fabric, set off with piping, can be sewn on the bottom edge of the blind to emphasize a scalloped effect. A pinked edge or a narrow border of lace can look charming, while, for a really feminine look, a frill can be extended all the way around the blind. With this trimming the blind should sit in front of the window recess; others can sit within.

Valances

VALANCES

Elegant or romantic, whimsical or theatrical, valances are a highly effective aspect of window dressing. They define the style of decoration and can be used to add individual flourish.

Valances vary enormously, from painted, carved or gilded wood to tailored strips of fabric mounted on a board and intricately draped, tailed and trimmed creations. Either on their own or conceived as an integral part of the window treatment, they are the ultimate decorative finish.

The Development of Valances

When divided curtains began to be used as a decorative feature in the interiors of the wealthier households at the end of the seventeenth century, it was not long before valances were adopted both to enhance and finish the window dressing and to cover up the plain rod and rings from which the curtains were hung. The valance, however, was not a sudden inspiration; it had existed in furnishing long before this development.

For many centuries, the dominant feature in the interior had been the bed — often a monumental four-poster curtained with tapestries, silk damask or worsted and surmounted by a canopy or tester from which the drapery was hung. Around the frame of the tester would be a richly trimmed valance, concealing the curtain rings and providing the excuse for lavish decoration.

The prime function of such hangings was to provide warmth and privacy. But, as the bed often stood in a room which was also used for dining, receiving visitors and general daily activity, hangings were also designed for public display and were an important indication of status. At their most luxurious, state beds in royal or aristocratic households were covered in drapery in sumptuous silks and velvets often trimmed with gold cords and braids and gathered into festoons to show off the quality of the cloth. When the new divided curtain style arrived, the idea for a valance was simply borrowed from the bed.

Divided curtains were initially made of lightweight silks and linens but with the adoption of the valance at the window, curtains and bed-hangings began to be coordinated, often in the richer, heavier fabrics of the latter. It took time, however, for the flamboyance of bed valances to be matched at the window; the first window valances were neat and plain while rigid valances of carved, sometimes gilded, wood were popular in many neo-classical interiors.

It took the French upholsterers of the late eighteenth-century Empire period to transform the valance into billowing, swagged drapery, defined by short and long tails at the edges and often trimmed by bows and rosettes at the tie-points. The neat, boxed valance disappeared in up-to-date interiors; the fashion was full-blown and artfully conceived, with valances integral to the whole style of window dressing rather than a mere finishing touch. This upholstery style spread across Europe and across the Atlantic to the United States.

ABOVE *Bed hangings provided much of the inspiration for early decorative window treatments. At the end of the seventeenth century, the new divided curtains were soon embellished with valances similar to those already used on four-poster beds. Lady at her Toilet (c.1670) shows a neat fringed valance, which coordinates with the bed curtains in colour and fabric.*

PRECEDING PAGES *Whether frilled or fringed, pleated or plain, a valance adds an elegant finishing touch to a decorative window treatment, and can also define a period atmosphere. A zig-zag valance, inspired by designs for the Royal Pavilion, Brighton, will instantly lend a touch of Regency style.*

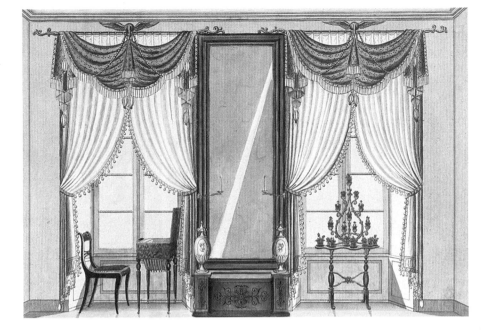

Simpler versions of Empire valances were created by draping fabric elegantly over a rod or pole. This drapery, sometimes criticized at the time for looking 'unfinished', was an extravagant and stylish way to show off and enjoy the quality and colours of a taffeta or damask. The valance would be looped across the top of a window and hung in delicate swathes on either side, one side perhaps being longer than the other. Or it would be gathered up into a rosette at the centre of the window and be swept in symmetrical festoons to the corners before being left to hang at the sides. Rich, colourful, lightweight fabrics were best suited to these treatments. To contrast, the curtains beneath were often made in simple white muslin or silk.

Early in the nineteenth century, heavily festooned or draped valances came to be used on their own as the sole window treatment. In 1808, Thomas Jefferson, ordering furnishing for Monticello, the house he designed in Virginia, specified: 'Drapery for the tops of 4 windows . . . no curtains being desired'. Then, in about 1840, a flat, shaped, fabric valance known as a *lambrequin* first appeared. It was produced in a variety of styles that reflected all the many revivals of the nineteenth century, but typically had an arched or squared top and elongated sides that reached almost to the floor, framing the window and screening the light. Intricate in outline as well as being tasselled and lavishly trimmed, the *lambrequin* featured in the elaborate, many layered window treatments of the time.

Other nineteenth-century valance styles included a flat, shallow valance hung behind the curtains and pole, the revival of carved and gilded wooden valances after 1850, which gave a look of grandeur to interiors, together with all types of complex, swagged hangings trimmed with tails, cords and fringes. There was also a fashion for 'raised drapery' in which loops of fabric were caught up over a second pole set above the main curtain pole.

In the Edwardian era, a move away from the elaboration and ostentation of high Victorian drapery provoked a vogue for the simpler pleated or gathered fabric valances, now a distinctive feature of 'Queen Anne' country house style.

ABOVE *A fringed valance was the fashionable finish in the eighteenth century for curtains that pulled up 'in drapery' to form swags and tails. This elaborate window treatment was as popular in America as it was in Europe, and forms the backdrop to this view of the house of John Phillips, a New Hampshire businessman, painted c.1793.*

LEFT *Empire-style valances, seen here in a contemporary illustration dated 1815–20, were often extremely elaborate affairs, displaying all the art of the upholsterer. Brightly coloured and lavishly trimmed, they make a striking contrast to softly draped lace curtains.*

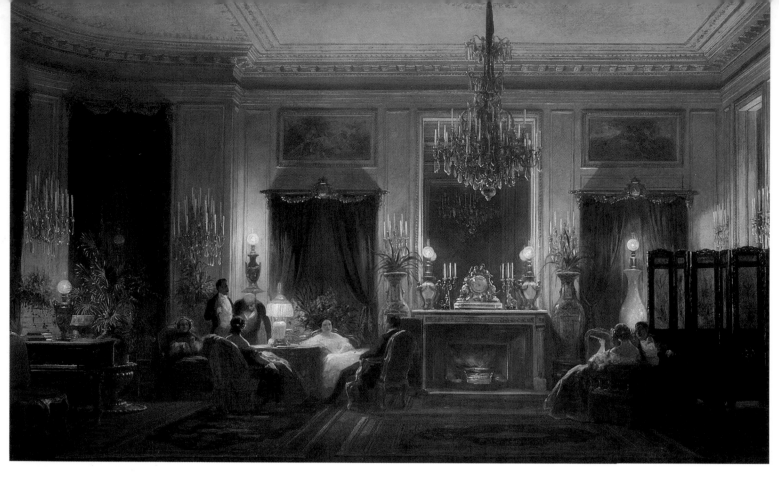

These were usually made in the same fabric as the curtains and were the width of the curtains; they were never used on their own but made a pleasing finish to the window treatment. Later on in the twentieth century, influential decorators such as John Fowler studied pre-Victorian examples for inspiration, recreating the draped and festooned styles of the Regency/Empire period from contemporary sources. These recreations provide the inspiration for many valance ideas now.

Valance styles

Choice of valance style should obviously be made both in the context of the effect you are trying to create and in conjunction with the rest of the window treatment. Flat or box valances, for example, work well with tailored curtain styles; ruffled or gathered valances have a softer look; and festooned or draped valances can work equally effectively on their own or as part of a grand, theatrical treatment. But, whatever style you choose, the depth of the valance is an important consideration. Although the Victorians used valances that extended as low as one quarter of the overall depth of the curtain, they are usually less dominant today. Festooned or draped valances may extend quite low, especially if used on their own, but sill-length curtains look better with narrow valances.

Another key factor is choice of fabric. The traditional approach is for the valance and curtain to be made out of the same material, but contrast is inherent in many valance styles. Simply because it is displayed flat, a patterned fabric will

Festoons and swagged valances gave way around 1840 to the lambrequin, a flat, shaped valance, intricate in outline and often tasselled, that framed the window.

58

FAR LEFT *All the richness and grandeur of the mid-nineteenth century is encapsulated in this view of the salon of Princess Mathilde. Carved and gilded valances make a glittering foil for deep green and crimson drapery.*

LEFT *A deep fabric valance in a Bloomsbury print has a triple pleat heading that blends with the curtain folds beneath – a charming thirties' look for French windows.*

BELOW *A smart, tailored effect is achieved with a serpentine valance, its neat box pleats mingling with columns of ivory fabric that fall simply but elegantly to the floor.*

not look the same on a box valance as it does made up into curtains. This dimensional contrast can be enhanced by choosing a plain, complementary colour for the valance or even by using a different pattern altogether. Fabric of a different weight can also be very effective; John Fowler designed a window treatment where the valance was of *toile de Jouy* and the curtains were striped cotton. Similarly, but in reverse, a festooned valance in a rich, heavy brocade, for example, looks dramatic with lightweight, semi-transparent curtains.

Gathered and pleated fabric valances

Using curtain heading techniques to gather or pleat the valance length, the valances in this category generally have a soft look. However, many different effects are possible, and depend on the fabric, the depth of the valance, the type of heading and the trimming.

A simple, gathered or pleated heading is traditionally used on valances made to match simply gathered curtains. The fabric of the valance is designed to flow into the folds in the curtains, which themselves drop vertically to the floor. With such a straightforward style, it is possible to use a flamboyant or strongly coloured fabric without being over-dramatic. A large-scale floral chintz in a drawing-room can be finished with a French-pleated valance with a pretty yet dignified result. The style also suits simple sprigged prints in attic bedrooms, striped lightweight cottons in kitchens and even plain fabrics in a modern utilitarian interior.

If you want a valance to suit linen curtains or even a linen blind – or any window treatment made in a stiffer fabric – a less fussy heading effect can be

ABOVE *Pencil-pleated for fullness, with soft curves and a narrow frill, valances in a small floral print lend a pretty, feminine look to a country house bedroom.*

RIGHT *A deep fabric valance, caught up with a tier of rosettes and trimmed with contrast binding, makes an elaborate heading for a graceful bow window in a formal drawing-room.*

achieved using box pleats on the valance. Decorative without being frilly or feminine, they are a pleasing alternative.

For further variation, the bottom edge of a gathered or pleated valance can be shaped. Scalloping, or a serpentine curve rising up in the centre can suit a softly pleated style; a stepped or toothed edge can emphasize the crispness of box pleats; a pinked edge looks best on gentle gathers.

Swagged and draped valances

Traditionally, swags and tails were the most formal and elaborate of valances, used predominantly in the entertaining rooms in the home. More recently,

however, these treatments have lent themselves to the decoration of all types of windows in all types of rooms. Wherever they are used, be it bathroom or reception room, they add distinction.

A swag is a sweep of fabric used horizontally and caught up at either end to create a semi-circular draped valance. This effect can be divided and repeated as you wish according to the width and height of the window. The effect achieved depends greatly on the amount and type of fabric; a full, deep swag is created using a great deal of fabric while a shallow swag uses a narrow width. The tails are, literally, what is left hanging on either end of the swag and can be either long and luxurious, simply cut short, or they need not exist at all.

Fabric valances can be shaped to accentuate a particular look: a classical style is achieved with a simple fluted valance, defined with deep green edging (top); for a romantic look curtains of sapphire blue chintz, overlaid with a layer of fine lace, can be matched by a softly shaped and gathered valance (centre); for a bold statement use exaggerated curves with a pencil-pleated valance in a large-scale floral print (above).

61

A soft drape of voile capped with choux

A double swagged valance

LEFT *Swagged and draped valances add a touch of sophistication to any curtain treatment. A full, deep swag creates a grand formal effect; for elegance with less formality, try a simple length of fabric draped around a pole and ending in a cascade of tails. Valances can also be divided and decorated with all manner of trimmings from* choux *to fringing or a contrast lining.*

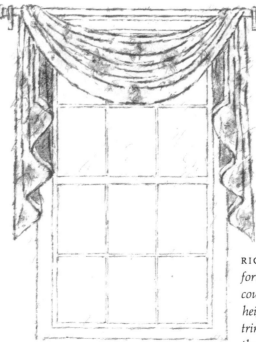

A swag with central choux *and cascading tails*

A draped valance with contrast lining

RIGHT *Swags need not be confined to the more formal drawing-room or dining-room. A country house bedroom gains distinction and height from vivid Regency-style valances trimmed with rosettes and bows, which make the perfect finishing touch to luxurious full-length curtains.*

LEFT *Swags and tails are highly effective where full-length curtains are not needed. Staircase and landing windows look dramatic framed by fluted swags in a crimson and grey geometric print.*

RIGHT ABOVE *An elegant yet light treatment for a drawing-room decorated in pastel shades is provided by deep double-swagged valances edged with the subtlest line of aquamarine fringing.*

RIGHT BELOW *Solid fabric valances provide a contrast to folds of fabric beneath. Deep curved box valances in jade green damask add to the formality of a dining room.*

There are various ways to use swags, and you can experiment and adapt to suit your needs. They can be divided into two giving a definite centre to the window, overlap each other or be stretched over a gathered valance ending in a choux on either side.

Swags can be adapted to all curtain and valance fittings, and are not difficult to achieve. They can be fixed onto a hidden wooden valance or hang beneath a carved or moulded wooden valance board. These both give a grand and formal look to the curtain treatment, and would suit a formal setting such as a drawing-room. On the other hand, fabric can simply be draped over and around a pole, ending either end in a cascade. In a fresh, light-coloured print with a contrasting lining, this effect can give definition to a window without making too grand a statement.

Although usually acting to enhance a curtain treatment, swags and tails can sit just as well by themselves at a window. They are particularly suitable where there is no need for curtains but the window still needs definition – for example, on a staircase where curtains might not be necessary. Or, in a bathroom, a length of fine muslin draped over a window from a central rosette will lend elegance and charm, without formality. If a window is too small for full curtains, follow the Georgian fashion of using a swagged valance with roller blinds hidden behind to be pulled down as sunshades or at night. Tails left to fall to the ground look like curtains although of course they cannot be drawn – a useful idea if you want to create the effect of curtains without going to the expense of all the fabric. Alternatively, just have one tail hanging down on one side of the window. This treatment can look striking when used on a pair of windows.

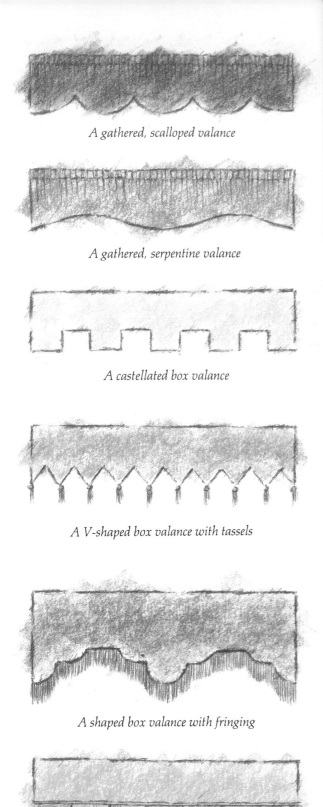

A gathered, scalloped valance

A gathered, serpentine valance

A castellated box valance

A V-shaped box valance with tassels

A shaped box valance with fringing

A box-pleated valance

Solid and architectural valances

Carved, gilded, painted, stained or varnished – solid wooden valances first became popular in the eighteenth century, since when they have been used either as a substitute for fabric valances or in conjunction with them.

Matching interior and exterior mouldings, mantelpiece decoration and the carving on picture frames, wooden valances can be as plain or as elaborate as desired. Lion heads, shields, leaf patterns, scrolls, rosettes, figures, Greek key designs – all these look impressive carved on a valance when they are tied in with other architectural and decorative motifs in the room. Otherwise, a motif such as a laurel wreath – perhaps set into the moulding or architrave – can be used as a device to hold up a gathered fan of fabric that then becomes the valance. Gilding the wood always adds a touch of grandeur.

An alternative is to make an 'architectural' valance in fabric. With bold rounded or pointed gothic arch or oriental-inspired shapes defining the hemline of the valance, the hanging 'columns' can be embellished with tassels or pompoms. The

FAR LEFT *A solid valance painted in classical style adds architectural interest to the full folds of burnt orange silk drapery.*

LEFT *A castellated valance, covered in a cream and oak brown print, is edged in darker brown to enhance its stylized shape – an appropriate treatment for a formal study with a masculine air.*

BELOW *For the effect of a valance where wall space is limited, a false valance sewn in with the curtain heading can provide an attractive solution. Here, the same fabric, picked out with a contrasting border, has been used to make a deep false valance over curtains hung from a traditional wooden pole.*

architectural shapes can pick out and emphasize existing architectural details or, if there are none, they can add them and add definition to a room. More idiosyncratic still, painting your own design on a flat-fronted valance adds an imaginative finish. None of these valances need very elaborate curtains or blinds as all the interest lies above.

In much simpler fashion, a plain box valance can be made in wood or board and covered in a fabric that either contrasts with or matches the curtains or blind and is used just to cover the heading. The advantage of this type of valance is that a large fabric design or pattern repeat can be displayed flat, without interruption.

False valances

A false valance is one that is attached to the front of the curtain, either suspended from the same pole or sewn in with the heading. The valance will accordingly open and close with the curtain. Use a contrasting fabric or the same fabric bordered for definition.

Lace, Muslin
and Voile

LACE, MUSLIN AND VOILE

Lace is inherently the most delicate and decorative of fabrics – both in itself, displaying filigree designs and an interesting texture, and as a filter of light, casting complex dappled shadows into an interior. Fine muslin and voile share its ability to filter light, but with softer, more muted results.

Besides providing privacy, screening views and cutting out glare, all three fabrics have many uses in window treatments. They can be supremely feminine gathered into curtains and romantic draped as a valance; lace is particularly eyecatching used flat as a decorative panel.

The Development of Lace and Muslin

Lace originated in Italy at the beginning of the sixteenth century as needlepoint lace, which was executed on parchment or fabric using a needle. Later in the same century, a certain Barbara Ullmann of Saxony is credited with the invention of pillow or bobbin lace, in which threads were twisted around a pattern of pins stuck into a pillow.

Countless Tudor portraits show the popularity of handmade lace as a luxury trimming on dress, adorning wrists, necklines and headdresses, but the art of lace-making did not reach its apogee in western Europe until the seventeenth and eighteenth centuries. The best, most intricate work came from Brussels, Mechlin, Valenciennes and Honiton, but was too much of a luxury to use on windows.

Muslin, however, has played an important role in window treatments since the Renaissance. Pictures of seventeenth-century Dutch interiors show embroidered muslin being draped extravagantly to frame a window. The Georgians made use of muslin for festoon curtains even in the formality of a panelled dining-room. The contrast between the flimsy muslin and the dark wood is surprising to our eyes but nevertheless very fetching.

It was in the late eighteenth and early nineteenth centuries that muslin came into its own. Not only used for undercurtains as a striking contrast beneath coloured curtains, it also became an essential component of the Regency asymmetrical drapery, with a muslin curtain drawn to one side of a window and a heavier curtain in a contrasting fabric to the other. Fine white, cream and even pink muslins were also used on their own, draped as extravagant valances over poles across tall windows, softening the light.

The mass production of loom-made lace during the Industrial Revolution of the nineteenth century brought about an exchange of the use of muslin for lace in interiors. With the Victorian passion for drapery and filtering light, often two panels of lace undercurtains would be crossed over and tied back as part of an elaborate window dressing. Heavy fabric curtains, valances, and swags and tails were all trimmed with tassels, pompoms and borders to be set off against the delicate lace. In addition to small repeat patterns, large pictorial designs were produced in lace and sometimes used in a panel beneath the undercurtains.

Lightweight muslin drapery was dramatically exploited in the asymmetric window treatments popular in the Regency period. This scheme for dining room curtains of 1810 shows a typically striking arrangement, with a rich crimson curtain contrasted with filmy muslin, crossed over and looped back behind embrasses.

PRECEDING PAGES *Delicate lace, fine muslin and voile, whether used as a decorative panel or softly draped, will all lend an exquisite translucency to a window view, their delicate patterns softly filtering the light.*

Loom-made lace remains popular as a window dressing in many areas of Europe, especially where strong light needs to be screened. It is common in Paris to look up from the street and glimpse through wrought-iron balconies long windows covered with old lace. (In cities it provides privacy too, of course.)

Lace is also widely used as part of the nostalgic vogue for Victoriana and for a country lifestyle. It looks charming lining cottage windows; in fact it adds old-world prettiness and interesting light effects to any interior.

Using Lace, Muslin and Voile

Made of cotton or linen threads, occasionally silk, lace is traditionally produced in white or ivory but it can, of course, be dyed any shade. Its great charm lies in its patterning. This can range from a rococo filigree, or floral posies and bows, to large-scale motifs. Handmade lace remains an expensive luxury and therefore of limited use for window treatments, but loom-made lace can look just as attractive and has many applications. The best-known varieties are Nottingham lace, woven on a jacquard loom, and Madras lace, a gauze-like fabric. They are available in wide widths for making into curtains, in panels, or in half-panels

ABOVE LEFT *A mid-nineteenth-century Berlin interior shows a generous arrangement of layers of palest pink and white muslin caught up in swags by fabric choux to create a stunning, shimmering effect that exploits the fabric's light-filtering qualities to the full. This delicate treatment is given definition by a rich green tasselled fringe and tie-backs.*

ABOVE *The charming effect of lace combined with printed fabric is seen in W. S. Gilman's study of a breakfast table conversation. Lace was used in many Edwardian interiors as a decorative addition for tables and chair covers as well as for windows.*

RIGHT *Lace panels combined with a simple roman blind make a sunny window treatment for an old-fashioned kitchen, casting delightful dappled shadows across the floor.*

BELOW *An overlay of lace adds a light, feminine touch to plain sapphire chintz curtains, its delicate pattern picked out by the light shimmering through the folds of the fabric.*

FAR RIGHT *An artfully draped muslin valance caught up with a rosette is a stylishly simple window dressing that underlines the light, fresh decoration of this blue and white bathroom.*

(known as *brise-brise*). Heavier laces can even be made into roller blinds.

Lace is a rewarding fabric with which to experiment. When hung beneath draped fabric valances or outer curtains, contrasts in texture are exploited. The traditional arrangement, reminiscent of Regency and Victorian treatments, is as full-length undercurtains, which can be drawn to prevent glare while the main curtains remain open. Sill-length tiers of café curtains, or curtains covering only the bottom half of a window can also be used with outer curtains, particularly if a large piece of furniture, such as a sofa, is set beneath the window.

Used on its own in straight panels, it transforms a window view with delicate patterning, rather like the etched effect of sandblasted glass. It can also be crossed over or used in overlapping layers – where the layers cross-pattern and intensify shadows. An alternative is to hang lace over a plain, unlined curtain; it modifies the underlying colour as light filters through.

Some of the effects of lace, although not all of the subtlety, can be achieved by using muslin, spotted voile, embroidered net, layers of tulle or gauze. All of these fabrics are open-weave and translucent and, like lace, are ideal for filtering light and creating a soft glow in an interior. One of the most elegant and pretty ways of utilizing them is to throw a length over a pole in simple loops with layers tumbling down either side, or to pull it up flamboyantly – Empire style. This softens the lines of a window frame in situations where curtains are not desired.

Lace and voile are particularly useful for screening French doors, and casement and dormer windows, where there is a need for privacy. The fabric can be fixed to the frame so that it does not obstruct the way the window opens.

Because it is so lightweight, a lace, muslin or voile curtain needs only the simplest heading. It can be gathered up softly and attached by small rings to a pole or given a cased heading and ruffled on a rod. Lace can look especially feminine in a bedroom suspended from a pole by ribbons, bows or loops.

Unusual Window Shapes

UNUSUAL WINDOW SHAPES

Certain windows may require special attention either because of their size and shape or because of their irregularity. When it comes to deciding on the treatment, there are no general rules as each window needs to be looked at individually and in context, but a little originality can add vitality and drama to what would otherwise be a standard solution.

Thermal windows

Graceful and elegant, thermal or Venetian windows are often associated with Georgian and Regency architecture, although the Victorians also used this design. Many are large and imposing, with decorative columns, pilasters and elaborate architraves, sited in important positions in hallways or at the heads of staircases.

There are a variety of ways thermal windows can be dressed so as not to hide the refinement of their shape or their features. One solution is to shape the curtain headings to follow the shape of each curve, by fixing them either to shaped tracks or directly to the frames. In the central window, divided curtains can be tied back high up, while single curtains can be swept to one side in the flanking windows.

If the window does not need to be covered, fabric valances can be used to emphasize the curves. Either gathered or flat valances can be effective, particularly if they are shaped so that they extend down the sides of the windows. For a very dramatic treatment, however, mix elements from different periods, with perhaps a gothic centrepiece and asymmetric swags and tails over side curtains drawn into bosses.

Roman and gothic arches

Roman arches need definition and are often best not covered at all, thus letting the light flood through to define their outline. Otherwise, any window treatment should fit in or around the arch so that the shape is always revealed and emphasized. Swags and tails or a festoon blind shaped within the arch, combined with a roller blind, are a good solution; a less formal effect can be achieved by looping a length of fabric over a pole above the window. Another idea is to treat an arched window as two separate shapes. The lower rectangular portion can be curtained and the rounded top permanently covered, perhaps with fabric gathered in sun-ray pleats to a central point and covered by a rosette.

A long series of arches might be best treated with a continuous draped valances extending across all the arches and individual pairs of arched gathered curtains tied back within each arch. Following Empire taste you might suspend a pole across the capitals of the columns, or at the point where the arches begin, and hang panels across. These can then each be tied in a knot and left to hang in a very dramatic way. Alternatively the panels could each be split centrally and the drapes scooped up to the sides of each arch.

Pointed arches or gothic windows were popular during the Victorian neo-

A Gothic arched window, a semi-circular Georgian fanlight or an elegant roundel require special attention when it comes to window treatments, but a little originality is all that is required to bring out the inherent beauty of many of these unusual shapes. Blinds can be used to great effect on arched windows, for example. A roman blind in a simple sprigged cotton covering a wide arched opening acts like an awning in this tropical garden room.

PRECEDING PAGES *The elegant curves of gently arched windows are further emphasized by loosely gathered curtains that are fitted into the curve itself.*

The elegance of this circular window with its fine glazing bars is highlighted by a delicate festoon set high above the window – a treatment which frames, rather than obscures. Bows decorate the top of the blind, picking out the apple-green sprig of the cotton print.

gothic revival and can pose special problems. Even the Victorians found this a difficult shape. One ingenious solution of the period was to cover the lower portion of the window with a blind painted to simulate stained glass. The best answer, however, is probably to set a pole well above the window so the curtains frame, but do not obscure, its shape.

Round windows
Round, oval and octagonal windows are not common today, but they were sometimes incorporated into Georgian houses, either lighting a stairway or piercing a wall at high level. Many of these windows are architectural features in their own right, composed of beautifully cut and shaped glass set in fine patterns by delicate wooden mouldings. There is often no real need to cover such a window, especially since this might well obscure the detailing. But the shape can be emphasized by means of a draped or festooned valance set above it and pulled up in the middle to form an arch.

Semi-circular windows or demi-lunes are also fairly rare. They tend to be located at the upper level of a house. One way to cover such a window is to fit curtains around the curve, on a curved track or fixed to the frame. These can then be reefed up to either side on cords. Festoon blinds are another solution.

Fanlights – semi-circular windows set above doors – are more commonplace, but almost never need to be covered. Originally they were designed to introduce light to hallways, particularly in terraced houses where there are no windows on the side wall. Many are decoratively shaped or composed of stained glass panels.

Bow and bay windows

The size, style and design of these curved and angled windows vary widely. Graceful curving bow windows, however, are generally fairly shallow. Bay windows – now seen as a hallmark of the Victorian terraced house – range from simple alcoves composed of three window panels to larger, almost room-sized projections that effectively involve covering a whole wall.

Today, tracks can be curved or angled to fit right around such a window, enabling it to be treated as a single unit; poles can also be angled. A pair of curtains hung from a track or pole that extends clear of the window frame will not cut out the light. Larger and deeper bays can be fitted with a curtain at each side and another pair framing the central section. When the curtains are open, the middle pair will make elegant columns of fabric defining the angles of the alcove.

There is no need, however, for curtains to hang directly over the window frames. A pole can be mounted on the wall at either side of the bow or bay so that curtains close off the alcove completely at night. Or false 'dress' curtains – lengths of fabric hung to resemble curtains drawn into a permanent daytime position – can frame the recess, leaving blinds or lace to cover the windows. Alternatively, fabric can be draped over a pole or a valance to frame the opening, while blinds cover the window, perhaps in a contrast colour or print.

French windows

French windows are glazed doors that usually open onto a balcony, garden or terrace. They are often combined with panels of windows at each side or above, essentially forming a window wall.

French windows can be treated in the same way as any large expanse of window, with the important condition that the doors must be able to open easily. Valances or curtains must be suspended high above the frame and curtains pulled back well clear so they do not catch in the sides of the doors. Lightweight curtains, gathered on narrow rods, lace panels or roller blinds can be fitted within the door frame, moving with it, with dress curtains added for extra flair.

Casement and dormer windows

The casement window is an ancient design; today, it is a style that evokes the country cottage. Casement windows open like doors, either inwards or outwards. Many are deeply recessed in thick old walls and they also tend to be fairly small, and paned or leaded, revealing little light.

LEFT *A deep bay window can be treated as a little room in its own right, with curtains placed to screen off the whole area. In this generously proportioned breakfast corner, the actual windows have only simple sprigged roller blinds, with the more expansive curtains running right across the entrance to the alcove.*

BELOW *Curtains for French windows should pull well clear, to allow the doors to open. Here a box pleated valance, with smart burgundy piping to match that of the curtains and tie-backs, is used to unify the window treatment and create a frame for the view into the garden.*

Any treatment for a casement should not interfere with the way the window opens. It should also be light and informal, in keeping with the overall style of the window. For casement windows that open inwards, curtains with cased headings can be fixed directly to the frame by rods at the top and bottom. If the window is deeply recessed but opens outwards, a hinged or swivel rod can be attached to the frame and the curtain suspended from it, so that it swings inwards independently of the window. Alternatively, curtains can be hung from a track or pole mounted on the wall in front of the recess.

Dormer windows, which project out from the roof line and have sloping sides, pose similar problems. There is often not enough wall area on either side for curtains to be drawn back clear of the window. Roman or roller blinds are simple and effective in such situations; for a softer effect, sill-length curtains can be fixed to the top of the frame and caught back with tie-backs. Hinged rods that swing clear of the window are also useful if light is a priority.

Skylights and attic windows

Set into the roof or high up a wall, many windows at the upper level of a house also slope, which increases the difficulty of covering them. Skylights over stair wells and rooflights in entrance halls do not need to be covered, but the light from a sloping window in an attic bedroom, for example, may be too stark without some means of controlling it.

A permanent solution is to filter the light by fitting lightweight curtains directly to the frame but greater flexibility can be achieved by installing roller blinds. Either way, a second rod set across the angle will hold the covering in place.

ABOVE *One of the cleverest solutions for dormer windows and deeply recessed casements is to hang the curtain from a rod which is hinged to swing clear of the window frame, maximizing the amount of light it admits.*

RIGHT *A demi-lune window in a Long Island bedroom shows how the balanced, classical façades of early American architecture often concealed a surprisingly haphazard arrangement of attic rooms behind their elegant windows. The curious segment of a window in this irregular little room has been framed as a square and hung with a cheerful striped sail curtain that is hitched up diagonally by day.*

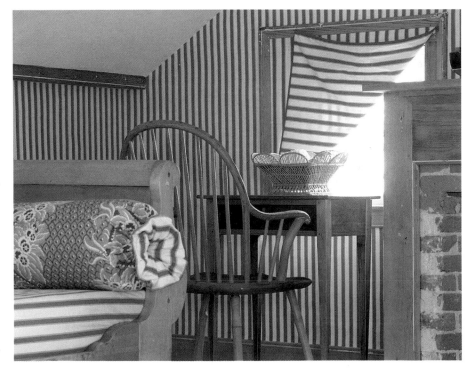

Where windows differ greatly in size or proportions, it is a good idea to accentuate rather than disguise this feature. The narrow window, between two much wider in scale, would not comfortably accommodate divided curtains, and has instead been hung with a festoon blind in the same fabric. Matching valances on all three windows tie the scheme together visually.

Corner windows

Windows that are set close together, meeting at a corner, are often best treated in the same way as an alcove. A valance can be placed across the corner to frame it and, combined with full-length curtains at either side, will provide visual unity. For a less formal effect, sill-length curtains are more suitable. If there is enough of a margin between the two windows, an alternative treatment would be to place a false dress curtain at the corner to give balance when the curtains are open.

Different-sized windows

Valances on their own or over curtains or blinds are a useful device for creating a unified look in a room where there are different-sized windows on the same wall. You can adopt the same treatment for the smaller one as for the larger ones, but modify it. So, where the larger window might have three swags across it, the smaller window need only have one. Otherwise, if space is a problem but you still want a flamboyant effect, use the same fabric in curtains for the larger windows and a blind, perhaps with dress curtains, for the smaller.

Decorative Details

DECORATIVE DETAILS

The correlation between changing fashions in dress and styles of soft furnishings is a fascinating aspect of the history of interior decoration. A well-known example is how neatly the Victorian penchant for covering everything in sight, including chair and table legs, corresponds to the layers of petticoats, crinolines and panteloons that modestly obscured female legs. In a similar way, soft, filmy Empire drapery was echoed in the graceful, flowing lines of the dress of the period, while curtains were often tied back at a height that corresponded to the 'Empire line' on dresses.

Many writers have taken this a stage further and noted links between fashion and furniture; even fashion and architecture, but the connection is most evident between costume and window treatments. The craftsmen who produced effects with drapery – the upholsterers – were often regarded in the same light as fashionable dress designers. Paris was regarded as the home of such skills during the Renaissance and on into the early nineteenth century, much in the same way as it has been the centre of *haute couture*.

As in dress, decorative details or accessories are often vitally important to the success of a look. They add a richness and a sense of flair and underline the particular qualities of a style, period or otherwise. They also provide the opportunity to contrast or complement the colours and textures of materials, adjust scale and proportion and generally provide the finishing touch that brings a window treatment to life.

Colour and design

Because such details as borders, fringes, braid, banding and piping are small in scale compared with the total curtain or blind area, they are an interesting way to add a vivid colour that might be overwhelming used as the main colour. The trimming can be in a toning shade, picked out from the main design, or it can make a striking contrast. At the beginning of the nineteenth century, for example, black tasselled fringes were combined with muslin drapery, creating a sense of drama and definition.

In the same way, design can be combined with design. A particularly effective way to do this is to line curtains or drapery in a different print, perhaps lighter and smaller in scale, and turn the lining over the leading edge of the curtain to display it as a decorative border. A plain curtain can be given interest by a border or tie-backs with a printed design or in a fabric of a different texture. Curtains or festoon blinds with a complicated design are usually suited to trimmings and frills in a plain matching or contrasting colour.

Texture

Textural contrast is another important way in which trimmings add depth and dimension to window treatments. For example, the dull lustre of gold cord makes it a natural foil for rich velvet or cotton sateen, while a soft cotton fringe throws the sheen of glazed chintz into relief. Some types of trimming, such as braid and

ABOVE *Decorative details can be used to enhance the proportions of a window, as shown in this view of a lady's boudoir by George Morland entitled* Dressing for the Masquerade, *c.1785. A gold tassel at the centre point of softly draped curtains reduces the height while creating a focal point above the half shutters. The eau-de-nil and cream striped fabric, edged with fringing and held back by gilded embrasses, is also used to upholster the painted chair, while the same colour scheme is used for the medallion-patterned wallpaper to create a fully coordinated effect.*

PRECEDING PAGES *A period fabric of multi-coloured stripes and flowers, taken from an eighteenth-century hand-painted silk, is edged with a crimson linen fringe, and held back with Victorian acanthus-shaped tie-backs.*

gimp, are inherently texturally interesting, as is lace, which has a softening effect however it is used.

Shape

Decorative details emphasize the cut and drape of fabric. Bows, rosettes or choux at the tie-points of swags or at the tops of pleats call attention to the fullness of the drapery; bias binding has a neat, tailored look; frills and flounces echo the ruched effect of festoon blinds.

Trimmings can also adjust the proportions of window treatments. A deep fringe along the lower edge of a curtain or valance will stress the vertical; the position and depth of tie-backs affect the apparent fullness of a curtain and its shape when it is pulled back.

Decorative schemes often took inspiration from the fashions of the day, and lavish fringing appeared on silk dresses and velvet curtain hangings alike in the nineteenth century. This scene of a society concert in a French chateau shows how trimmings add a special richness to fine drapery. Heavy gold fringing and tassels combine with lavish crimson curtains and swagged valances to splendid effect.

LEFT *The opulence of these floor-sweeping curtains in soft rose pink is accentuated by a wide brocade border and plump tassels which add a touch of grandeur.*

ABOVE *A swagged valance of floral-patterned chintz is given a simple edging of smoke blue bias binding, a colour picked out from the main design.*

Types of Trimming

Along with an eye for colour and textural possibilities, choosing trimmings and decorative details demands a sense of stylistic appropriateness. A wide range of traditional trimmings is available today, often coordinated with existing fabric ranges, and dressmaking trimmings extend the scope even further. Antique shops can be a good source for original details, but rosettes, bows and other fabric accessories can easily be made at home.

Banding and edging

Different types of border braid, gimp, lace edging, ribbon and bias binding (also used to make piping) are the trimmings generally used to outline and define the shape of curtains, valances and blinds, as well as other decorative details such as rosettes, bows and tie-backs. They can also be inset into the fabric to make panels or used to emphasize fringes and frills.

Borders in contrasting designs or colours work to unify a treatment. A border along the bottom edge of a fabric valance could be matched by borders along the bottom edge of curtains and perhaps also along the inside edge of curtains. Similarly, it is very effective to run a border along the valance and echo it in the tie-backs, leaving the curtains plain.

Trimmings such as gimp and ribbon neaten and cover unfinished edges. They are equally appropriate on feminine styles of window dressing, following the curves of frills and flounces, as they are on formal swagged curtains and even on plain roman blinds. Whatever the style of the room, if they are used to pick out colours used elsewhere, they create a pleasing sense of unity.

Fringes

Fringes inevitably call to mind the rich drapery of the Victorian era, when they were used to trim not only curtains, blinds and valances, but also cushions, lampshades, upholstery and tablecloths. But they were a feature of earlier window treatments, too; tasselled and knotted fringes were applied to muslin drapery and deep block or bullion fringes to swags and tails in the eighteenth and early nineteenth centuries.

Designs vary widely, from those which suit grand, elegant treatments to less formal varieties. Block fringes – fine, dense and often quite deep – have a silky appearance and are usually composed of two or more different colours or threads. They may have the effect of elongating a curtain or blind, and can be used when an impression of height is deliberately being emphasized.

Bullion fringes are heavier, made of thicker, twisted cords in wool or cotton; they too look rich and opulent and suit large and emphatic window treatments. The heavier the fabric, the heavier the fringe should be.

Then there are a whole range of knotted and tasselled fringes, both narrow and deep. Pompom fringes are yet another charming alternative. Quite a number of these fringes are made in two contrasting colours, to complement colours in particular fabrics.

Fringes can be used to provide sharp colour accents. A deep gold bullion fringe extends the effect of a gilded valance while a second white cotton fringe sets off the swag beneath in a smoke blue and white fretwork design.

Frills

Frills, ruffles, flounces or gathered fabric edging soften the lines of curtains and valances and promote a light and pretty look. Frills look best on the leading edge of full gathered curtains, on valances and around festoon blinds, where they emphasize the overall style of dressing.

Although usually coordinated with the main curtain or blind fabric, frills can be made in a strong contrast colour, pattern or even texture — as in the case of lace frills. They range from narrow borders that can be ruffled, scalloped or pinked to deep, skirted flounces edged in yet another contrast.

Frills combine well with other trimmings. Piping or braid can be used on their edges to set them off; bows, rosettes and other flourishes can be made up in the same fabric and attached in the corners or at the centre of a valance. And frills have a look of extravagance that can be heightened by shaping, fan pleating and even by the use of double frills — frills on frills — for the ultimate decorative effect.

Flourishes

Equally enjoyable and exuberant, there are a variety of decorative flourishes that are traditionally associated with particular styles of window treatment. Regency festoons and swagged drapery, for example, were typically decorated with fabric rosettes or bows, set at the tie-points of the swags or along the top of a valance or curtain on the pleats, if they are far enough apart. Variations on this theme were choux — gathered, crumpled fabric trimmings similar to rosettes but usually

ABOVE *Picking out a colour from the floral print, a narrow china blue pleated frill makes a sympathetic edging for a festoon blind.*

RIGHT *The ultimate extravagance of double frills adds charm and femininity. Here, the ruffled edge of a delicate ribbon-patterned fabric is emphasized with a second ruffle in rose pink.*

larger and in three dimensions rather than flat. All of these can be adopted successfully today, either as part of a period effect or to add a special touch to simple cased or gathered headings.

Tassels were a popular way of decorating 'festoon curtains' in the eighteenth century; they then reappeared in the late nineteenth century combined with sweeping loops of cord. The Victorians favoured particularly elaborate effects; tasselled cords were occasionally used to secure arrangements of dried grasses and even Japanese fans.

Today, tassels can be used hanging on their own to make a punctuation point at the corners of formal drapery, or tasselled cords can be looped and draped to accentuate rich folds of fabric. Cord or decorative rope might be used alone and led or draped along the top of a valance to be knotted at the centre.

LEFT *Simple cased curtains are given a decorative flourish with frills, rosettes and bows edged in a coordinating rose pink.*

TOP Choux, *made from a tube of fabric lightly tucked with stitches to give the required shape, provide effective accents along a swagged valance.*

ABOVE *Cords and tassels add a sense of movement and luxury draped in simple loops over bordered moiré curtains.*

ABOVE *Fabric tie-backs can be used in a variety of ways – decoratively shaped in a scallop design, or perhaps in the form of soft bows given a contrast lining, frilled in a coordinating colour or given a pinked edge.*

LEFT ABOVE *A shaped fabric tie-back, contrast edged in sage green and decorated with a fabric choux, adds wit and style to light, floral print curtains.*

LEFT BELOW *A twisted silken cord enhances the elegance of aquamarine curtains striped with apricot and given a subtle line of fringing.*

RIGHT ABOVE *A gilded embrasse adds a touch of opulence to a softly draped candy pink curtain, caught back with a twisted silk cord.*

RIGHT BELOW *A knotted cord with sumptuous tassels complements the style and colours of a floral chintz for a formal look.*

Tie-backs

Tie-backs are far more than the practical means by which curtains are held open. Their position, depth and design not only dictate how much light is let in through a window but also the shape and apparent fullness of the curtains when drawn back.

The current vogue for positioning tie-backs is at one-third the total height of the window dressing, or at the height of the sill. Although these are generally acceptable proportions, variations either side of these standards can create a range of effects from the severity of tightly drawn back drapery to the Regency style of curtains loosely looped back lower down. The depth and style of a tie-back can vary from wide bands of fabric to cinching cords, knotted and tasselled, depending on the style of the curtains.

Fabric tie-backs

Fabric tie-backs can be formal and tailored, pretty and frilled, decoratively shaped or plain. They can match the curtains or be made of a contrasting material, either plain or patterned. If the valance contrasts with the main curtain fabric, it creates a unity if the tie-backs match the valance.

Edges can be shaped and trimmed to coordinate, too: either straight, pinked, scalloped or finished with a frill. And plain tie-backs can be dressed up with a rosette or bow or even small, lined tails to match the larger tails above.

Cord tie-backs

Rich and sophisticated, cords or ropes are also popular choices for curtain tie-backs. These often look best combined with full-length heavy drapery. Tasselled cords were particularly favoured by the Victorians, although Marie Antoinette adopted this detail at Versailles as early as 1792.

Cords are available in different widths and in a wide range of shades, from thick, silken gold ropes to narrow colour-coordinated cords, knotted and trimmed with tassels.

Solid tie-backs

For a grand window treatment, especially for formal draped effects, solid brass hold-backs or *embrasses* can promote a look of elegance. These details also have a particular Empire or Regency flavour and coordinate well with the trimmings of that period such as rosettes and bows.

Antique shops are a useful source for original examples, but good reproductions of these traditional details are also widely available. The two principal types are brackets and decorative bosses. Brackets can be plain or elaborate, even displaying moulded Prince of Wales feathers. Bosses simply catch back the weight of the curtain on their arms. The boss itself is often ornately decorated – sometimes rosette-shaped.

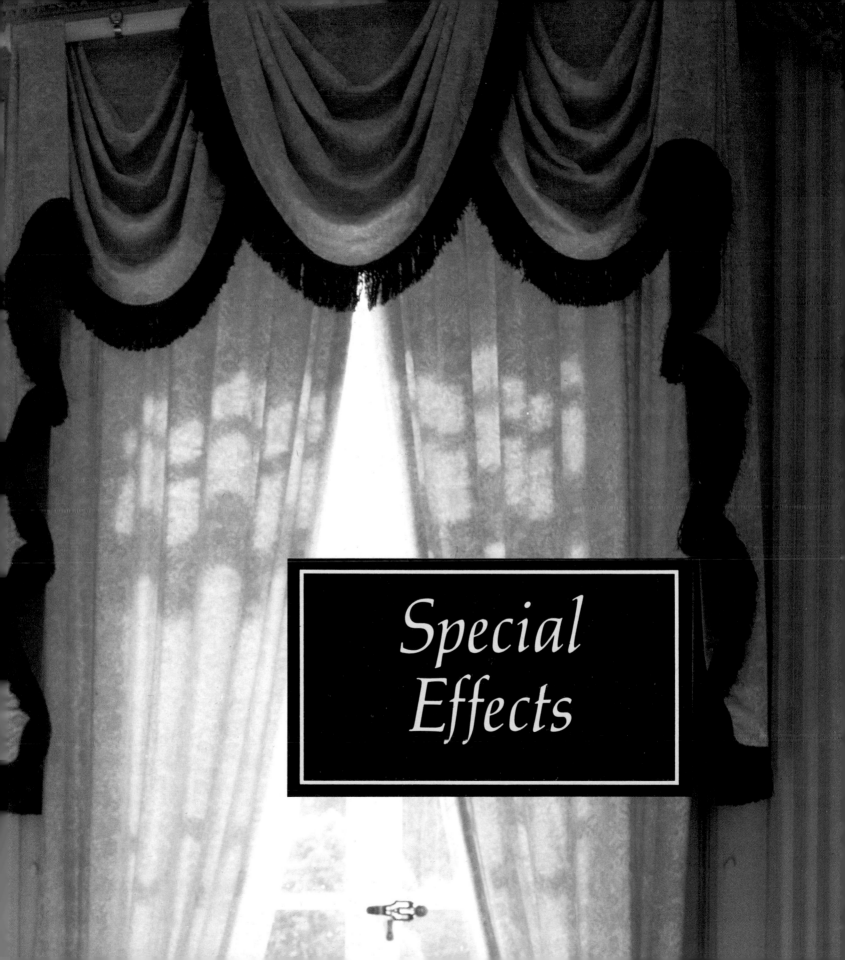

Special Effects

SPECIAL EFFECTS

Creating a successful window treatment always demands a certain degree of imagination but, like all forms of interior decoration, you can take a step further and enter the realms of special effects and pure fantasy.

This chapter gives ideas and suggestions to inspire you to recreate or adapt an extravagance from the past. It could be a Napoleonic style with asymmetric valance treatments on gilded poles, or a Regency indulgence with its oriental influences and royal whimsy, or a romantic creation with a feminine festoon of chintzy rose bowers and waterfalls of lace. You can draw from many different sources and combine them to dramatic effect.

The best way to stimulate or tempt your imagination is by visiting country houses and gaining ideas from the window treatments of past centuries, or visiting museums and art galleries where paintings of period interiors provide a wealth of information. Whether you have a penchant for the romance of the rococo or for the grandiose of the baroque, there is something to suit every personality and taste in the amazing creations of the past.

Fantasy

Fantasy is about going beyond the limits, breaking the rules and mixing the unexpected to create the unpredictable. It involves being bold enough to put the most flamboyant of window treatments into the most simple of rooms.

Windows in a Victorian terrace house, for example, can be adorned with rich, heavy curtains and draped, fringed valances, recreating an opulent and dramatic interior akin to something in the Victorian era. The same treatment can equally be applied to a more modern style of window. Naturally the choice of print plays an important part as it determines the overall effect. Delicate floral prints used in the same flamboyant way create a more feminine version of the theatrical.

With fantasy the aim is to dazzle and excite the eye. The two masters of this art were the monarchs Louis XIV and the Prince Regent who took everything to extremes, indulging their whims in extravagant interior decorations. The Prince Regent's dazzling touch was seen in the Rose Satin Drawing Room at Carlton House (now destroyed) where magnificent red satin damask curtains and swagged valances adorned with gold fringing on every possible edge dominated the room. The effect was pure theatre, achieved by the magnificence of colour, the opulence of fabric and the sheer outrageous audacity of the idea.

The Victorians created their fantastical gothic interiors by combining seemingly disparate elements. They boldly covered oriental-shaped valances with contemporary prints and combined them with velvet curtains and lace. Such contradictions created drama. Curtains were further exaggerated by embellishment with luxurious trimmings, which created a fantastical effect in their own right. An elaborate mix of frills, fringing, rosettes, ribbons and waterfalls of fabric can lift any window treatment well beyond the ordinary.

ABOVE *Recreating the richness of the Victorian interior, curtains in a warm, dark, floral print are topped with a deep swagged valance edged with a deep bullion fringe. Period treatments are an excellent source of creative inspiration.*

RIGHT *Layer upon layer of soft muslin cover these bedroom windows, recalling the romance of Empire style. Both curtains and valances have the same light, airy quality, while the valances are given a delicate defining edge with a white knotted fringe.*

PRECEDING PAGES *The full luxurious curves of swagged valances are dramatically emphasized by deep fringing – a lavish, audacious effect.*

Similarly, a row of windows can be covered very extravagantly in 'continuous drapery'. This is a term for a valance that travels from one end of a set of windows to the other, crossing an area of wall in between. The length of drapery looks very luxurious simply by virtue of the amount of fabric involved, and the overall effect is often enhanced by the addition of decorative details such as trimmings, tassels, cords, rosettes and tails. A variation on this idea is for each window to have its own small swag or set of swags, and the points between them to be decorated with short lined tails or bows hanging in front of the valance.

Taking fantasy to the extremes, a window treatment can be extended around the room to create a tented effect. The window cannot then avoid being the focal point as it is the only opening in a room of fabric. The 'tent' can be achieved by draping the walls with fabric or papering them to match the curtains and just continuing the valance on around the cornice. The valance will determine the character of the effect – whether it be grandiose swags for formality or zig-zags with tasselled ends for an interpretation of the gothic. More of the fabric can be gathered up to create the impression of a canopy over the ceiling.

ABOVE *Shaped fabric valances form a decorative double cornice around the walls of this Parisian tented boudoir. The curtain treatment and valances, repeated over doorways and chimneybreast alike, are given an edging of brilliant emerald green, and rich tassels complete the exotic 'Turkish' ambience so fashionable in the nineteenth century.*

RIGHT *In this private retreat, the window treatment is extended around the room so that walls and ceiling alike are enclosed in a cocoon of lavishly pleated fabric.*

FAR RIGHT *Complex swags and tails, trimmed with a bobble fringe and large choux, look light and elegant in a softly draped moss green and cream chintz.*

The same idea in a more modified form can be created by repeating the curtain treatment over doors, alcoves, arches and chimney breasts, creating mirror images throughout the room. The result could be light and ethereal with layers of lace echoing the window treatment or rich and dark with luxurious drapes of brocade.

Combinations

Many window treatments of the past consisted of more than one layer: heavy outer curtains in a rich fabric to provide warmth and privacy at night; lighter inner curtains in lace or muslin to filter light and provide privacy during the day; roller blinds to draw down against the glare. Combining different types of treatment meant combining the practical advantages of each while also creating drama.

The practical advantages of combining treatments are just as valid today. And, more importantly, some of the richest and most sophisticated effects can be generated by building up layers of window dressing. Combining treatments offers the opportunity to exploit contrasts – of style, texture, print, colour and transparency. One of the main advantages is that you can often add to what already exists and yet totally transform the window.

The secret to successful window combinations is to use the various elements in unusual ways. For example, an Austrian festoon blind can be used purely decoratively as a valance over curtains; this combination was fashionable in the eighteenth century and was later adopted by the Victorians. The festoon blind can be operational or erected purely for effect; it can be treated formally with heavy fabric and lavish trimmings, or femininely with a pretty floral cotton print.

Such valances can also be combined with roman or roller blinds which, in any case, were originally intended to act as sunshades by day with the festooned blind coming down by night. These combinations were popular during the eighteenth and nineteenth centuries in Europe and the colonies, where less elaborate window dressings were preferred. The combination of a festoon and lace curtains works in the same way, with the lace filtering and shading the light. It is surely the most feminine of combinations and suitable for a morning room or bedroom.

Festoon blinds work equally well under a fixed valance. This combination evokes magnificent splendour for more formal rooms and elegant hallways. A swagged or shaped valance embellished with bullion fringing echoes the swags of the blind when pulled up, giving a strong contour to the window. The effect can be further enhanced with curtains or decorative dress curtains caught back with tassel tie-backs.

Dress curtains are an important feature in that they add interest and give definition to a window that does not need curtains for practical reasons. Windows with working shutters that close to keep out the light may still need this softening effect.

ABOVE *Tailored roman blinds are combined with flowing dress curtains to create a very stylish effect. Colours and patterns complement each other too.*

LEFT ABOVE *Rich crimson drapery, heavily fringed, frames the view into this Victorian conservatory, creating a sense of theatre. The lightness of delicate lace panels behind provides dramatic contrast.*

LEFT BELOW *A plate from a Parisian magazine, c.1814, shows the combination curtain treatment fashionable at that time. Sprigged voile curtains are topped with a continuous valance of vivid yellow silk, while the deep scalloped border lends definition.*

When using a combination of styles it is always exciting to use a combination of prints — perhaps a large floral chintz for the curtains and a smaller cotton floral for the blind. Or use a stripe vertically on the curtains and horizontally on the valance. Be bold and create innovative and eye-catching combinations. Experiment with colour, contrasting a plain-coloured valance with another plain colour for the curtains. The aim is to delight and tease, so that the window demands attention. Pick out a colour from the main print with which to contrast and coordinate, and carry the idea over to the trimmings.

Combinations of texture make equally dramatic effects. Keep the heavier fabric in the valance treatment and the lighter fabric, like lace or muslin, below. This idea is particularly appropriate in hot climates where a mass of draperies is undesirable but the effect of a curtain is required.

Experiment further by combining lace with muslin or printed voile to create an ethereal quality in a room as well as a subtle contrast of textures. Or place lace over a heavier fabric so that, instead of light filtering through, the print and colour of the base fabric is discerned. Woven damask, silk, velvet or chintz give the best effects with very striking contrasts.

In and Out
of the Window

IN AND OUT OF THE WINDOW

Fabric dresses a window, links it with the overall decorative scheme and offers great scope for exploring the potential of colour, pattern, texture and period detail. But window treatments are only part of the picture. Room arrangement, the use of mirrors, plants and flowers, can all have an important effect on the way the window works as a focus of interest.

Viewed from the interior, windows draw in the outside world. But windows are also viewed from the outside, where they express the architectural character of a building and provide tantalizing glimpses of the inside. There are a number of ways in which the exterior of windows can emphasize style and setting.

Inside out

Room arrangement

Traditionally, the twin focal points of the interior have been the window and the fireplace. Before electric light and central heating, there were strong practical reasons why rooms should be arranged to make the most of these features.

Windows have long provided the daylight necessary for everyday activities such as reading, letter-writing, sewing, music-making, card-playing and so on. In the seventeenth century, as soon as windows could be made relatively large and transparent, the layout of rooms and arrangement of furniture was oriented to benefit from the improvement in the quality of light. The lightweight furniture typical of the later Regency period, for example, with its elegant, tapering legs, was designed to be portable. Informal groupings were set up during the day around the windows and then reassembled at night around the fire.

Windows provided more than light, however. One characteristic of early nineteenth-century middle-class Biedermeier interiors – a northern European development of Empire style – was a shallow platform sited directly beneath the window. On this would be placed a chair and writing or sewing table, making a discreet vantage point from which to watch the world go by. In other, stricter cultures, windows were – and are – designed specifically for this purpose. Muslim screens in the Middle East and South American *miradores*, or street windows, allowed the women of the household to maintain their privacy while satisfying their curiosity.

Today, despite the fact that, in theory, electricity makes any interior arrangement possible, windows remain an important focus of attention because they allow the simple enjoyment of light, views and fresh air. The layout of a room can be organized so that the window is a focal point. In a room with a window on two facing walls, furniture can be aligned along the axis or arranged into two units. Tables could be placed immediately in front of the windows, and chairs and sofas ranged in two circles, at least one of which will probably also include a fireplace within its radius.

An angled bay, recessed window or window set in an alcove can be treated as

ABOVE *The window has long been the focus of any interior – purely for practical reasons before the advent of electricity. This Victorian party clusters around an open window to make the most of the last of the daylight as they read their sheet music.*

PRECEDING PAGES *A room composed entirely of windows, the conservatory, where house meets garden, was much loved by the Victorians, who had romantic sensibilities for the natural world. It is still the ultimate location for idling away balmy afternoons.*

a little room in itself; many provide adequate space for a sofa or a side table, a desk or even a dining table. By its nature, being mostly glazed, an alcove is a perfect space for daytime reading, whilst also being very romantic for evening meals – half in and half out of the garden.

Creating an illusion

Mirror glass has been a popular way of maximizing the effect of windows and increasing available light since the Renaissance. From the late seventeenth century onwards, mirrors and their frames played an increasingly important part in the decoration of rooms in Britain. The margin of wall between pairs of tall Georgian windows was often filled with a mirror, while, sometimes enclosed in glass frames, a mirror also formed part of the increasingly elaborate architectural structures over and around fireplaces. In this position they reflected light and views but also provided the symmetry sought in neo-classical designs.

At first, the frames were made of ivory, silver, ebony or tortoiseshell or were veneered with marquetry but, from the late seventeenth century carved wooden frames became more common, usually crafted to match the decoration of the room. As tastes changed, the frame would be removed and replaced to make full use of the expensive mirror glass.

Nowadays we use mirrors for very similar reasons. Light in a room will be increased by placing a mirror opposite a window; it also seems to increase the size of a room. A mirror will create the illusion of an additional window if it reflects a view of trees, flowers and sky. Chosen carefully, period frames will add further interest and reinforce the atmosphere you want to achieve with your window treatment.

ABOVE LEFT *Mirror glass is a time-honoured way of creating a sense of light and space. Use a looking-glass to reflect an elegantly curtained window and the view that it frames.*

ABOVE *Oriental cultures have conceived some highly decorative window treatments that allowed women to maintain their privacy while satisfying their curiosity. J. F. Lewis's fanciful Victorian interpretation of life in a Cairo harem shows an exquisitely carved pierced window screen creating an invitingly cool secluded interior.*

103

RIGHT *Foxgloves in soft pastel shades bring the atmosphere of the country to this hallway, drenched with afternoon light.*

BELOW *Wide, scrubbed oak window ledges make a sunny platform for terracotta pots of flowering plants, a perennial feature of cottage interiors as captured in this rustic scene by F. G. Cotman (1850–1930), entitled* One of the Family.

Indoor plants and flowers

The window is a natural site for plants and flowers of all kinds, not merely because conditions here are optimum for their survival but also because plants emphasize the link with the outdoors. Pots of geraniums, hyacinths and even hydrangeas on sills are a recurring theme of the charming Biedermeier window compositions, but it was from the middle of the nineteenth century that plants were increasingly used to decorate rooms.

The Victorians prized plants because they brought the atmosphere of country life into the homes of the increasing numbers of city dwellers. Also, their shapes and rich green colours made interiors look exotic. Ironically, the gloominess of many late Victorian interiors somewhat restricted the choice.

When introducing plants and flowering plants into a room it is important to consider existing conditions so that plants can survive and flourish. Windows vary in the amount of light they reveal. Shaded, high or heavily screened

Citrus trees flourish in this arched hallway, a simple means of linking outside and inside. If grown in containers, and overwintered in a sheltered spot, they can be grown in cool climates too, their glossy dark green leaves and fragrantly-scented flowers forming an indoor oasis.

windows may create conditions that are too dark for sun-loving species but large, light windows may amplify the sun's rays to the extent that others are in danger of scorching. Some varieties will do better in the steamy atmosphere of a bathroom than elsewhere, but all plants need careful watering because central heating and air conditioning create a dry atmosphere.

Just as in any other aspect of interior decoration, plants are chosen for their form, texture or colour – with the added dimension of scent. They can also be used to emphasize the style of decoration. A row of bright geraniums looks appropriately cheerful on a sunny kitchen window sill; gardenias, orchids and cyclamen have a delicate beauty that suits a classically elegant drawing room; a hanging basket overflowing with lush ferns emphasizes the period qualities of a study decorated in a Victorian style. Direct inspiration can even be taken from the curtain fabric and flowers and plants can be matched with the pattern of a floral chintz or sprigged cotton.

IN AND OUT OF THE WINDOW

RIGHT *A window filled with flowers graces a country entrance hall – the simple curtains are in a print whose floral richness is echoed in bunches of real flowers, both fresh and dried, which pick up the same tones of rose, moss green and sapphire blue.*

BELOW *A ceramic pitcher of garden flowers, placed in front of an open window, will add freshness, subtle colours and a delicious fragrance to a room.*

An interesting and popular alternative to plants are the many sweet-smelling varieties of dried flowers now available. Arranged into baskets for a kitchen or hallway, into vases and urns for a reception room or into posies for a bedroom, they look welcoming and pretty on window sills or on the floor by a window all year round. The greatest luxury of all, however, is a plentiful supply of fresh cut flowers. These bring any room alive with their delicacy and subtle colours. Whether you place a simple bowl of old-fashioned roses or a great vase of tall, brightly coloured dahlias and foliage in a window recess, fresh flowers always look particularly bright and pretty with the light behind them. They enhance any interior and smell delicious.

Outside in

The elevation

The style and distribution of windows on the facade or elevation of a building emphasizes its architectural character, which is why modern replacement windows look out of place in an older property. Today it is possible to restore, maintain or even replace windows so that they remain in keeping with the period or style of a house.

Some windows, especially on older houses, are set off with period features — perhaps by pediments, mouldings, pilasters or exterior shutters. These features can be added when appropriate, to enliven very blank, bare walls, and painted if necessary. Painting a window trim white or a light colour will make the window seem larger; black or dark grey, on the other hand, will make the window seem smaller and more recessed.

One aspect of window treatments that is often ignored is how they appear from the outside. Coloured and patterned fabric linings add a great deal of interest. It is a good idea, however, to ensure that such treatments do not clash with the colour of the walls. A pink lining set against a red brick facade, for example, could make the complete look a little overwhelming.

The other aspect of window treatments that is visible from the exterior is the style of curtains or blinds. Again, it enhances the look of a house when they are extravagant or in period. Swagged valances, festoon blinds and curtains with tie-backs look particularly elegant from outside.

Window gardening

Gardens are often best conceived as extensions of the room from which they are viewed. This particularly applies to the planting of window boxes, containers for balconies and terraces and the planting of beds directly beneath a window. Window gardening is gardening for inside as well as out. Looking at the window from the outside is just as important as looking at the view from inside. The two perspectives should complement one another.

As with indoor plants, light conditions will dictate which plants will do best in a particular location. Soil conditions can be improved — and, in the case of

Exterior views should be planned as carefully as any interior decoration. The neat, geometric planting of box hedges is perfectly in keeping with an elegant, restrained Georgian façade.

FAR LEFT *An ornamental vine frames this leaded casement window while a window box, filled with a tumbling profusion of lobelia, begonias and poppies in subtle shades of mauve, cream and coral, adds a decorative touch.*

LEFT *Heavy mauve blossoms of wisteria cascade down over the balcony of a French villa, its sunny, sheltered wall providing just the right environment for this beautiful ornamental climber.*

container plants, strictly controlled – but the aspect of the house is unalterable. Nevertheless, plants can be used to set off and frame windows in a great variety of ways. The style of container is important too. Terracotta urns, painted or seasoned wooden boxes and tubs are all suitable for window and garden use.

The elegance of a formal facade demands a balanced, ordered display, using plants that can be pruned or trained. Shrubs and trees are generally most successful. Bay, box and yew trees can be clipped into classical shapes such as pyramids and spheres and used to frame a balcony or terrace. Fruit trees can be trained and box hedges pruned into geometric topiary or grown to frame parterres or knot gardens, providing a strong framework for flowering plants.

Window boxes should be treated as stretches of flowerbed, with plants arranged in groups, not lined up in rows. Containers can be planted seasonally, with spring bulbs such as snowdrops, crocuses, narcissi and tulips giving way to summer annuals – pansies, petunias, lobelia and sweet william. Even larger plants such as *Alchemilla mollis*, stocks or field flowers like poppies and scabious look pretty in a box.

For informal window gardens, the emphasis is less on shape and symmetry and more on colour, clutter and surprise. Plants which climb, trail and frame all suggest the encroaching, overflowing garden. Hanging baskets can be planted full of fuchsias, lobelia, pelargoniums and nasturtiums; trellises can support wisteria, clematis, climbing roses or morning glory; tubs and troughs full of cottage flowers and even wild flowers can be grouped on a patio or balcony.

And perhaps the ultimate way to transform the view from a window is to plant a tree. Slow-growing deciduous trees such as flowering crab apples and mulberries are well shaped and have colourful foliage, flowers and fruit, which makes them ideal for screening windows too close to the street while providing visual delight the year round.

ABOVE *The paintbox gaiety of multi-coloured pansies makes a cheerful splash of colour against the weathered walls and window frame of this ancient cottage.*

Laura Ashley Shops

In addition there are a further 297 retail outlets in the United Kingdom, Europe and the Pacific Basin.

CANADA

Sherway Gardens,
ETOBICOKE,
Ontario,
M9C 1B2

2110 Crescent Street,
MONTREAL,
Quebec,
H3G 2B8

136 Bank Street,
OTTAWA,
Ontario,
K1P 5N8

2452 Wilfred Laurier
  Boulevard,
STE-FOY,
Quebec,
G1V 2L1

18 Hazelton Avenue,
TORONTO,
Ontario,
M5R 2E2

1171 Robson Street,
VANCOUVER,
British Columbia,
V6E 1B5

Bayview Village Shopping
  Center,
2901 Bayview Avenue,
WILLOWDALE,
Ontario,
M2K 1E6

Mail order:

Laura Ashley,
5165 Sherbrook Street W.,
Suite 124,
MONTREAL,
Quebec,
H4A 1T6

UNITED STATES

Crossgates Mall,
120 Washington Avenue
  Extension,
ALBANY, NY 12203

139 Main Street,
ANNAPOLIS, MD 21401

514 East Washington Street.
ANN ARBOR, MI 48104

29 Surburban Square,
ARDMORE, PA 19003

Lenox Square,
3393 Peachtree Road,
ATLANTA, GA 30326

Perimeter Mall,
4400 Ashford-Dunwoody
  Road,
ATLANTA, GA 30346

Highland Mall 1224,
6001 Airport Boulevard,
AUSTIN, TX 78752

Pratt Street Pavilion,
Harborplace,
BALTIMORE, MD 21202

203 Beachwood Place,
26300 Cedar Road,
BEACHWOOD, OH 44122

200–219 Riverchase
  Galleria Mall,
BIRMINGHAM, AL 35244

180 Town Center Mall,
BOCA RATON, FL 33431

83 Newbury Street,
BOSTON, MA 02116

23 Church Street,
BURLINGTON, VT 05401

Charles Square,
5 Bennett Street,
CAMBRIDGE, MA 02138

Carmel Plaza,
CARMEL-BY-THE-SEA,
CA 93921

Charleston Place,
130 Market Street,
CHARLESTON, SC 29401

The Mall at Chesnut Hill,
199 Boylston Street,
CHESNUT HILL, MA 02167

Watertower Place,
835 N. Michigan Avenue,
CHICAGO, IL 60611

The Citadel,
750 Citadel Drive E. 2008,
COLORADO SPRINGS,
CO 80909

1636 Redwood Highway,
CORTE MADERA, CA 94925

3333 Bristol Street,
South Coast Plaza,
COSTA MESA, CA 92629

Galleria 13350 Dallas
  Parkway,
Suite 1585,
DALLAS, TX 75240

423 North Park Center,
DALLAS, TX 75225

Danbury Fair Mall C-118,
7 Backus Avenue,
DANBURY, CT 06810

1439 Larimer Street,
DENVER, CO 80202

The Kaleidoscope at the Hub,
555 Walnut Street,
Suite 218,
DES MOINES, IA 50309

Twelve Oaks Mall,
27498 Novi Road,
Suite A,
DETROIT, MI 48056

Galleria Shopping Center,
3505 West 69th Street,
EDINA, MN 55435

11822 Fair Oaks Mall,
FAIRFAX, VA 22033

West Farms Mall,
FARMINGTON, CT 06032

2492 E. Sunrise Boulevard,
Galleria Mall,
FORT LAUDERDALE,
FL 33304

213 Hulen Mall,
FORT WORTH, TX 76132

58 Main Street,
FREEPORT, ME 04032

Saddle Creek Shopping
  Center,
7615 W. Farmington
  Boulevard,
GERMANTON, 38138

Glendale Galleria,
GLENDALE, CA 91210

Woodland Mall,
3175 28th Street S.E.,
GRAND RAPIDS, MI 49508

321 Greenwich Avenue,
GREENWICH, CT 06830

Riverside Square Mall,
HACKENSACK, NJ 07601

Ala Moana Center 2246,
HONOLULU, HI 96814

The Galleria,
5015 Westheimer,
Suite 2120,
HOUSTON, TX 77056

1000 West Oaks Mall,
Suite 124,
HOUSTON, TX 77082

Fashion Mall,
8702 Keystone Crossing,
INDIANAPOLIS, IN 46240

The Jacksonville Landing,
2 Independent Drive,
JACKSONVILLE, FL 32202

Country Club Plaza,
308 W. 47th Street,
KANSAS CITY, MO 64112

The Esplanade,
1401 W. Esplanade,
KENNER, LA 70065

White Flint Shopping Mall,
11301 Rockville Pike,
KENSINGSTON, MD 20895

7852 Girard Avenue,
LA JOLLA, CA 92037

Pavilion in the Park,
8201 Cantrell Road,
LITTLE ROCK, AR 72207

10250 Santa Monica
  Boulevard,
LOS ANGELES, CA 90067

Beverly Center,
121 N. La Cienaga Boulevard,
Suite 739,
LOS ANGELES, CA 90048

Louisville Galleria 109,
LOUISVILLE, KY 40202

2042 Northern Boulevard,
Americana Shopping Center,
MANHASSET, NY 11030

Tysons Corner Center,
1961 Chain Bridge Road,
MCLEAN, VA 22102

The Falls,
Space 373,
8888 Howard Drive,
MIAMI, FL 33176

The Grand Avenue,
275 W. Wisconsin Avenue 5,
MILWAUKEE, WI 53203

208 City Center,
40 South 7th Street,
MINNEAPOLIS, MN 55402

Ridgedale Center,
12401 Wayzota Boulevard,
MINNETONKA, MN 55343

The Mall at Green Hills,
2148 Abbot Martin Road,
NASHVILLE, TN 37215

260–262 College Street,
NEW HAVEN, CT 06510

333 Canal Street,
151 Canal Place,
NEW ORLEANS, LA 70130

979 3rd Avenue,
NEW YORK, NY 10022
(Decorator Showroom)

398 Columbus Avenue,
NEW YORK, NY 10024

4 Fulton Street,
NEW YORK, NY 10038

21 East 57th Street,
NEW YORK, NY 10021

2164 Northbrook Court,
NORTHBROOK, IL 60062

224 Oakbrook Center,
OAKBROOK, IL 60521

Owings Mills Town Center,
10300 Mill Run Circle 1062,
OWINGS MILLS, MD 21117

320 Worth Avenue,
PALM BEACH, FL 33480

469 Desert Fashion Plaza,
123 North Palm Canyon
Drive,
PALM SPRINGS, CA 92262

12 Stanford Shopping
Center,
PALO ALTO, CA 94304

221 Paramus Park,
Route 17,
PARAMUS, NJ 07652

401 South Lake Avenue,
PASADENA, CA 91101

1721 Walnut Street,
PHILADELPHIA, PA 19103

Biltmore Fashion Park,
2478 E. Camelback Road,
PHOENIX, AZ 85016

20 Commerce Court,
Station Square,
PITTSBURGH, PA 15219

1000 Ross Park Mall,
PITTSBURGH, PA 15237

2100 Collin Creek Mall,
811 No. Central Expressway,
PLANO, TX 75075

419 S.W. Morrison Street,
PORTLAND, OR 97204

46 Nassau Street,
Palmer Square,
PRINCETON, NJ 08544

2 Davol Square Mall,
Point & Eddy Street,
PROVIDENCE, RI 02903

Crabtree Valley Mall,
4325 Glenwood Avenue,
RALEIGH, NC 27612

South Bay Galleria,
1815 Hawthorne Boulevard,
Space 172,
REDONDO BEACH, CA 90278

Commercial Block,
1217 E. Cary Street,
RICHMOND, VA 23219

Regency Square Mall,
1404 Parham Road,
RICHMOND, VA 23229

Northpark Mall,
1200 East County Line Road,
RIDGELAND, MI 39157

531 Pavilions Lane,
SACRAMENTO, CA 95825

74 Plaza Frontenac,
ST LOUIS, MO 63131

St Louis Center C-330
515N. 6th Street,
ST LOUIS, MO 63101

Trolley Square,
SALT LAKE CITY, UT 84102

247 Horton Plaza,
Space 265,
SAN DIEGO, CA 92101

University Town Center,
SAN DIEGO, CA 92122

1827 Union Street,
SAN FRANCISCO, CA 94123

563 Sutter Street,
SAN FRANCISCO, CA 94102
(Decorator Showroom)

Suite 1224,
North Star Mall,
7400 SAN PEDRO,
San Antonio, TX 78216

Le Cumba Galleria,
3891 State Street 109,
SANTA BARBARA, CA 93105

Valley Fair Mall,
Suite 1031,
2855 Stevens Creek
Boulevard,
SANTA CLARA, CA 95050

696 White Plains Road,
SCARSDALE, NY 10583

F-331 Woodfield Mall,
SCHAUMBURG, IL 60173

405 University Street,
SEATTLE, DC 98101

The Mall at Short Hills,
SHORT HILLS, NJ 07078

20 Old Orchard Shopping
Center,
SKOKIE, IL 60077

Stamford Town Center,
100 Greyrock Place,
STAMFORD, CT 06902

139 Main Street,
STONY BROOK, NY 11790

Old Hyde Park Village,
718 S. Village Circle,
TAMPA, FL 33606

2845 Somerset Mall,
TROY, MI 48084

Utica Square,
1846 21 Street,
TULSA, OK 74114

1171 Broadway Plaza,
WALNUT CREEK, CA 94596

300 D Street SW,
Washington, DC 20024
(Decorator Showroom)

3213 M. Street NW,
Georgetown,
WASHINGTON, DC 20007

85 Main Street,
WESTPORT, CT 06880

Bullocks Westwood Shops,
10861 Weyburn Avenue,
WESTWOOD, CA 90025

422 Duke of Gloucester
Street,
WILLIAMSBURG, VA 23185

290 Park Avenue North,
WINTER PARK,
FL 32789

740 Hanes Mall,
WINSTON-SALEM, NC 27103

279 Promenade Mall,
WOODLAND HILLS, CA 91367

108 Worthington Square
Mall,
WORTHINGTON, OH 43085

Mail order:

Laura Ashley Inc.,
1300 MacArthur Boulevard,
MAHWAH, NJ 07430

Index

Numbers in *italics* refer to illustration captions

Acknowledgements

All illustrations are reproduced courtesy of the Laura Ashley Archives with the exception of the following (figures in **bold** refer to page numbers):

Title page Arcaid (photo: Lucinda Lambton); **6–7** Private Collection/Bridgeman Art Library; **8** A. F. Kersting; **9** George H. Hall; **10** Bulloz; **11** below Bulloz; above Tim Woodcock; **12** GAC, on loan to The Tate Gallery, London; **13** left and right Tim Woodcock; **14** left The Tate Gallery, London; right Tim Woodcock; **15** Townley Hall Art Gallery and Museum, Burnley/Bridgeman Art Library; **16** Victoria and Albert Museum, London; **17** Arcaid; **22** Musée de Strasbourg/Weidenfeld & Nicolson Archives; **25** below Weidenfeld & Nicolson Archives (photo: Rick Kemp); **29** Tim Beddow; **32** Bridgeman Art Library; **33** Victoria and Albert Museum, London; **34** Historisches Museum der Stadt Wien/Weidenfeld & Nicolson Archives; **35** Fine Art Photographic Library; **46** Victoria and Albert Museum, London; **47** left Richard Green Galleries; right Roy Miles Fine Paintings Ltd/Bridgeman Art Library; **56** The Minneapolis Institute of Arts; **57** left Victoria and Albert Museum, London; right Hood Museum of Art, Hanover, USA; **58** above Bulloz; below Weidenfeld & Nicolson Archives; **60** left and right Mimi Packenham; **66** Isabella Forbes and Fiona Skrine/valance design (photo: Simon Wheeler); **70** Mary Evans Picture Library; **71** left Schlossmuseum, Darmstadt; right Southampton City Art Gallery; **84** Bridgeman Art Library; **85** Bulloz; **96** left Victoria and Albert Museum, London; **98** below Victoria and Albert Museum, London; **102** Private Collection/Bridgeman Art Library; **103** right Victoria and Albert Museum, London/Bridgeman Art Library; **104** left Walker Art Gallery, Liverpool/Bridgeman Art Library; **107** Weidenfeld & Nicolson Archives (photo: Clay Perry); **108** Fritz von der Schulenburg; **109** left Brigitte Thomas; right Image Bank

The publishers and Laura Ashley would like to thank Zafer Baran for the artwork illustrations.